The Love of Jesus
and the
Love of Neighbor

KARL RAHNER

The LOVE of JESUS and the LOVE of NEIGHBOR

Translated by Robert Barr

CROSSROAD · NEW YORK

1983

The Crossroad Publishing Company
575 Lexington Avenue, New York, N.Y. 10022

Originally published as *Was heisst Jesus lieben?*
© Verlag Herder Freiburg im Breisgau 1982
and *Wer ist dein Bruder?*
© Verlag Herder Freiburg im Breisgau 1981

English translation copyright © 1983
by The Crossroad Publishing Company

Printed in the United States of America

Library of Congress Cataloging in Publication Data

Rahner, Karl, 1904–
The love of Jesus and the love of neighbor.

Translation of: Was heisst Jesus lieben? and Wer ist
dein Bruder?
1. Jesus Christ—Person and offices—Addresses,
essays, lectures.   2. Brotherliness—Addresses, essays,
lectures.   3. Love (Theology)—Addresses, essays,
lectures.   I. Rahner, Karl, 1904–   . Wer ist dein
Bruder? English. 1983.   II. Title.
BT202.R32313   1893   232   82–23523
ISBN 0-8245-0611-1   0-8245-0507-0 pbk

Contents

Who Are Your Brother and Sister?   63

WHAT DOES IT MEAN TO LOVE JESUS?

Preface

In the following pages we shall attempt to say something about a Christian's relationship to Jesus. Even before we begin, to be sure, it is clear that in such a short space we can only give intimations, indicate directions.

The first part of this little meditation consists of a reworking of an article I published in the Vienna monthly *Entschluss: Zeitschrift für Praxis und Theologie* 36(1981):3–18, 23–24. The second part originally appeared in *Geist und Leben* 53(1980):405–16, and is based on an address given to Austrian physicians. This is why the two parts overlap just a bit, and also why the second is not written in exactly the same style as the first.

Nevertheless, I hope that the lines of thought I present here, which I have revised for their presentation in this book, will serve the reader in good stead. For after all, the subject is one on which there will never be enough written by a Christian for Christians.

Karl Rahner

Introduction

What does it mean to love Jesus? Here we are dealing with a subject that it is useless merely to read about. Of course, one can simply read through the material—it can be done quickly, and one will have the impression of knowing it all by heart ahead of time as far as the words are concerned. It will be a matter of making the author's connections. But this is a fairly easy matter too, at least as far as a general idea of these connections is concerned. And then one will feel one has understood the sentences and propositions.

But there is another way of reading the same material. Now the words will first of all signify a challenge—a challenge to allow what the words say to summon up the content of one's own life experience, and so afford them entry into one's mind and heart.

We can think we understand words like *love, fidelity, patience,* and so forth on first hearing. But we will also have to admit that we only really understand these words by gathering together our life experiences while listening to them—slowly, patiently, ever and again listening to our own lives—just as someone might collect fresh spring water in a beaker as it wells up slowly out of the earth. Only a person who reads these words in this second way can really understand them and experience any effect. And it is only in this second way that they are meant.

Once the reading is done in this way—so as to listen to the experiences of our own lives right along with the reading—then it is no longer a matter of great importance that the words be written with all the exactitude of a mathematical formula. We can improve on the words, in search of a better expression for the same thing, even when the words only point more or less vaguely in the right direction.

Surely it cannot be otherwise. For even if such words as these were to be just as exact and just as understandable as words can possibly be, and even if we were to stipulate that of course they are subject to criticism and improvement, still in the last analysis they are religious words, and as religious words they ultimately denote the incomprehensible God and his ineffable mystery, so that the only way they could be out-and-out false would be to be perfectly "clear" and no longer open to quiet, loving improvement by the reader and translation into his or her own life.

The one who has written these lines hopes he has performed a service to a living, vital relationship with Jesus, as beseems the truth. He has no wish to conjure his readers with lyrical words, and so instill in them a love for Jesus. No, he only asks them to think about this love.

PART I

On Love for Jesus

1 · Some Preliminary Clarifications

Mere Human Being? Abstract Idea?

Our relationship to Jesus is an altogether complex reality. It seems to me that there are two misunderstandings to be avoided in the relationship of the "Christian," as he or she is called, to Jesus today. One is the mistaken notion that Jesus was just a human being —a person full of enthusiasm for life, yes, an unselfish human being—but just a human being. Here we have "Jesuanity" rather than Christianity, and suddenly we no longer see any basic reason why the person for young people to seek out as an inspiration and example in their lives should have to be precisely Jesus of Nazareth rather than somebody else. After all, they really do not know very much about him, usually, and they are presented with an entirely arbitrary selection of New Testament texts from which to paint their own, very subjective picture of him. Would a modern, Jesuanical Jesus like that preach eternal damnation, for instance?

The other one-sided picture of Jesus might be labeled "Jesus as an Idea." Now I readily admit that when I was young I read Paul more than the synoptics—precisely because there, in Paul, the magnificent Christ-idea was to be seized in all its clarity and immediacy. In Paul, in John, the eternal Word of God comes right down from heaven. Here is the one who has created the world from the beginning and holds it in his hand. And now this Absolute Logos, the World-Reason, appears concretely in Jesus of Nazareth, bears witness to itself, and accomplishes the deed of redemption on the cross, thereupon to return to the glory of God the Father. And there it more or less disappears, indistinguishable from the absolute God. Jesus Christ, ever so easily, is but a kind of algebraic symbol for God's absolute self-bestowal upon the world, so that if you do not arrive at this figure, or if you substitute another quantity for it, you have not actually lost anything. We forget: It is precisely in this concrete Jesus, and only in him, that what this symbol refers to has actually come to pass. And forgetting this, we find it easy to present Jesus Christ as, for example, the Omega of a cosmic evolutionary process.

As for calling upon Jesus or turning to him, Jesus as a historical person is well-nigh forgotten. One turns to that living, comprehensive World Principle that is with God by its very nature and calls it Jesus—as if out of a historical tradition that is all but coincidental—while really scarcely understanding any longer why this eternal, loving, cosmic Power of God that redeems us should be called precisely Jesus. One could almost say we are confronted here with the evolution of a Christianity experienced indeed as marvelously liberating and charging the world with ultimate meaning—but no longer including, or needing to include, Jesus of Nazareth.

Indeed, one might well ask: Where, in the other great religions, is the equivalent of this redemptive cosmic Logos, which we Christians happen to call Jesus, but which perhaps in another religion is denoted by another name for exactly the same thing?

The Risk of a Relationship
If we want to avoid both of these misinterpretations and distortions in our relationship to Jesus, which evidently we must—if we want to see Jesus neither simply as a human being and nothing more, nor as an abstract idea—then we must meet certain conditions, both theoretically and in the slow unfolding of existential practice. This is what we should like to speak of next. We shall expect, in doing so, to come in contact with still deeper, more basic problems of Christology.

First, it seems to me, one must come to grips with the fact that human beings necessarily commit themselves, entrust themselves, to others, and that indeed they must do so. This self-opening of one's own personhood to another, this handing-over of oneself to someone else, admits of the greatest variation in intensity and form. One form it can take, perhaps the clearest, is that of marital love. Here, unconditionally (at least in a certain sense), a human being confides himself or herself to another person. Only if one thus abandons oneself, and lovingly sinks into the other, does one succeed in finding oneself. Otherwise, a person languishes in the prison of his or her own selfishness.

Now, there is a very important aspect in this basic, factual occurrence of human existence that calls for our special attention. And it is this: A reasonable, responsible self-abandonment requires grounds upon which one feels called to abandon oneself to another, and thereupon justified in doing so. But these grounds, always and necessarily, are more tenuous and more problematic than the act of abandonment itself, the act of self-commitment in its absoluteness. Or, to put it the other way about: The act of self-commitment to the other has a radical, absolute, unconditional quality by no means adequately founded or based on the antecedent grounds for that act. This is the fact, and a human being can see, in his or her human existence, that it can scarcely be otherwise. One must have reasonable grounds for abandoning oneself to another—for committing, for entrusting oneself to another. And yet, in this self-abandonment, once all antecedent considerations, verifications and demands of reasonableness and legitimation are posited—one ventures more, and *must* venture more, than these grounds seem to justify.

Every trusting, loving relationship to another human being has an uncancellable "plus" on the resolution-and-decision side of the balance sheet—as over against the reflective side, the side that tallies up the justifiability and reasonableness of such risk and venture. Here we can draw our first conclusion with regard to the subject under consideration: a genuine love relationship to Jesus.

One can pursue exegesis and biblical theology, one can launch a thousand investigations into the historical figure of Jesus—one can seek to bring to light just what Jesus said, how he said it and how he meant it, what happened to him, how his environment reacted to him, and how he understood himself. One can research what we term his miracles with all precision and all exactitude. One can attempt a more exacting psychological analysis of why and how his first disciples, after his death, came to the conviction that he had risen again. All these considerations and investigations are good and necessary (to be sure, according to each person's opportunity for perception and verification, in the thousand different ways in which this sort of legitimation of a human conviction can be undertaken). But always there remains that "plus" on the side of the freedom to take a risk—on the side of love, precisely—in a truly Christian relationship to Jesus; for this relationship is above and beyond all these historical, exegetical and critical sciences (and of course also above and beyond the historical witness of tradition and the Church concerning Jesus). Only when Jesus himself is accepted and loved in himself, over and above one's own knowledge about him—Jesus himself, and not our mere idea of Christ, nor our mere willingness to brook the lucubrations of historical science—only then does a true relationship to him, the relationship of an absolute self-abandonment to him, begin.

Bridge to Someone Far Away

Before we attempt to portray our peculiar, unique, and radical relationship to the unique person that is Jesus of Nazareth, in an absolute commitment and an unconditional love, there is still one preparatory consideration calling for our attention. As we have already said, our relationship to Jesus must involve more than an abstract idea of Christ—otherwise we should be simply hypnotized by our own idea of him and riveted to that, instead of loving a concrete, actual human being.

But after all—or so it seems at first—the concrete Jesus is cut off from us, is he not, by geographical space, by the distance of history and culture, and by the span of two thousand years. Can one love a person in earnest when that person is that far away? When one seeks to do so, does one not necessarily fall back into an enthusiasm for an *idea* of Christ, for one's own self-invented ideal of the selfless human being?

The normal Christian, not considering all these questions quite so precisely, will at first simply reply: But this Jesus is alive today. He is risen. We can find him with God. And therefore a loving, radically immediate, unique relationship to him holds no insuperable difficulties.

This is all very important, of course. In fact, it is basic to our

Christian understanding of a relationship to Jesus. Were he not the Resurrected One, the Saved One who abides with God, the one returned to God and there achieving his definitive survival and being, precisely in the incomprehensible infinity and ineffability of God—then our love would surely be no more than the quest (ultimately, a meaningless quest) of an ideal in history's past. Indeed, were it to be taken as adequate by itself alone, the rather too hasty answer we have just heard would present us with a brand-new difficulty of its own: The blessed in heaven, whom we believe to be saved and in God, appear to us to be just as removed—at an infinite distance—as if they had disappeared into the incomprehensibility of God himself, and were no longer distinguishable from him.

We cannot delve more deeply into this difficulty here. Rather we must simply recall that God is "a God of the *living*," as Jesus himself tells us he is, and that the departed are everlastingly current, and so can be, and are, really near to us in their silent love. But is this nearness not, once again, precisely the nearness of the God who saves them and keeps them, but also hides them? And does not this same thing then apply to Jesus?

Many men and women lovingly seek to reconstruct within themselves, as it were, extraordinary personalities of history. There are people who observe a cult of Napoleon. There are people who honor Goethe in such fashion that he has great importance and significance for their lives. Such people seem to have succeeded in bridging the historical distance between themselves and their heroic idol of the past. Such phenomena should by no means by undervalued. One could certainly say that a person who had simply let none of the heroes of history into his or her life, who practiced no hero worship whatever in any sense, who had no capacity for dialogue with the figures of the past, would somehow be stunted, diminished, in his or her own humanity.

But evidently it will not be enough for us to say that we bridge the historical, cultural and temporal distance to Jesus simply and solely in this way. There must be something more to it than that. Were we *only* to say that Jesus now lives with God, that he still exists, that we can still call on him, as Stephen did before his death— "I see the heavens opened, and the Son of man standing at the right hand of God" (Acts 7:56)—then, as we have said, we would have a basic prerequisite for an immediate relationship to Jesus, a prerequisite that is absolutely necessary and important. But then there would still be the question whether, with this "eternal Lord of all," as Ignatius Loyola calls him, his bygone, now past history actually still has a meaning for us—or whether we are really just falling back once more into a cult of an abstract Christ-idea.

Diversity as Task

If we cast a backward glance over our own religious history we cannot exclude such a danger a priori. When a Teilhard de Chardin speaks of Christ as the Omega of world history, the question arises at once whether this Teilhardian Christ-All as goal and ground of all evolutionary history can still seriously have anything to do with Jesus of Nazareth. But how—without simply appealing to an ancient and approved hero cult, but nothing more than that, and yet without watering this Jesus down into an idea of some sort —how can we make this relationship to Jesus comprehensible for today and tomorrow?

Actually, we notice we have the same problem with respect to the cultus of the saints (which has an altogether official place in the Catholic Church and may not be allowed to be dismantled by cries for reform). When I honor Francis of Assisi, I not only strike a relationship with his exemplary life of long ago. Nor do I simply cultivate a Franciscan idea of the person who loves God and the world unselfishly. I also pray to Francis of Assisi. I call to him in the definitive redeemedness of his existence. This reflection shows us that the problem of an immediate, genuine relationship to another person who is seemingly far removed from us historically is a more general one than merely one of our relationship to Jesus. This circumstance permits us to examine things the other way about and apply this general Christian attitude and deportment to the special question of our relationship to Jesus.

Human beings seek nearness to one another. When they are in one another's direct physical presence and seek to love one another in these circumstances, they seek to exist not only in a physiological contact of flesh on flesh, but to render such contact, when it is to be meaningful, the expression of a really total, personal, fully mutual and reciprocal exchange of love between them. Here we have a mystery that we cannot hope to solve at this point in our discussion—if indeed it can be solved at all.

What happens, then, when two human beings love? What happens when, despite their diversity, two persons succeed in existing in such mutual exchange of themselves, such mutual communication and sharing, that it can be said that their love makes them *one*? Is there really such a thing as this uniting, unifying love—a love that genuinely surmounts all the seemingly insurmountable barriers, that spans all the gulfs of separation thrown across its path by the physical, material (and existential, too) diversity of two distinct subjects?

This is yet another question that cannot be answered in detail here. But one thing is altogether clear. When we observe human love, we see that this same basic diversity between two people, this basic division separating them, obtains even when they are very near one another, even when they actually seek to unite themselves bodily. They are different, they are distinct. Their respective existence is not given a priori as if it sprang from one source and origin. With all their physical and physiological proximity, the two remain diverse, distinct. They fall back, or at least they seem to fall back, into separation again, even when, in the act of supreme love, they seem to have achieved a unity, a oneness. But (and now we come to the point) even though this basic diversity obtains between two lovers, indeed abides in the very basis of their love, and yet does *not* cause their love not to be—difficult as it may be to explain the coexistence of diversity and unity in love speculatively—then neither can a seemingly great distance in space and time between two persons who seek to love, and actually do love, betoken an impossibility for love. After all, even before its encounter with this spatial and temporal difficulty, love must face a much more radical difference—and experience shows it is perfectly capable of doing so. For this earlier, greater difference is given in the very ground, the root, of this love. Indeed, their difference is actually to be reaffirmed in this love—for the lover loves and affirms the other precisely *as* other, certainly not seeking simply to absorb the beloved into his or her own peculiar way of being.

Now if such love, always and in all situations, in its very roots, is beset with this difficulty—a difficulty that constitutes precisely one of the tasks of love—then it cannot mean death for this love if it has to come to grips with an at least apparently great spatial and temporal separation. Lovers naturally seek the greatest possible nearness and palpable bonds of affection—at once the alleviation and the expression of their love's intensity. But they love each other across time and space. Such a love knows that it is yet but on the way to the goal of definitive union in love—that it must bridge, in fidelity, the chasm still provisionally sundering the lovers. But to say that love must founder, or no longer be, when a like distance in time or space separates lovers would be to vacate the true and genuine essence of love.

Hence we must say: One can love Jesus, love him in himself, in true, genuine, immediate love. To be sure, we can and must unhesitatingly stipulate, in this case, that the one who is loved is really alive with God. To be sure, we may stipulate and grasp by faith that it is this Jesus, on his own initiative, out of the depths of the divinity that is his and that preserves him in life, who seizes the initiative of his love for us, and through what we call grace—the divine gift of love for God and Jesus—makes this love for him possible for us.

The Courage to Throw Your Arms Around Him

Under these two conditions and stipulations of ours, however, it is really possible to love Jesus, across all space and time. We read his biography. It is not the biography just of someone's past. This biography has taken on definitiveness in his resurrection. We read Holy Scripture in the way two lovers gaze at one another in the living of their daily life together. We feel and experience in the depths of our own existence, what this concrete human being— who has not simply sunk away in the shadowy anonymity of God after all—has concretely to say to us. We allow ourselves really to be told something by him that otherwise we should not have known for our life. We find ourselves face to face with a synthesis, an indissoluble one, between norms that are ever valid and Jesus as their unique model. This synthesis forms the basis of a consequence for our lives that is something more than an acknowledgment of the exemplar of a self-evident norm. The imitation of this person by no means implies his demotion to the status of mere exemplar of principles we have already adopted. Jesus becomes, in this love of ours for him, the concrete Absolute, in whom the abstractness of norms, and the insignificance of the purely contingent individual, are transcended and overcome.

A little story may help show what I mean. Once I was having a conversation with a modern Protestant theologian, whose theories, to a normal Catholic Christian like me, necessarily seemed rather rationalistic—very much an existential "Jesuanity" and no longer really having a great deal to do with the Jesus of the normal Christian faith. At one point I put in with, "Yes, you see, you're actually only really dealing with Jesus when you throw your arms around him and realize right down to the bottom of your being that this is something you can still do today." And my theologian replied, "Yes, you're right, of course—if you don't mean it too pietistically."

I think one can and must love Jesus, in all immediacy and concretion, with a love that transcends space and time, in virtue of the nature of love in general and by the power of the Holy Spirit of God.

At this point in our considerations we have only sought to make it in some measure clear that the spatial, cultural, and temporal distance between Jesus and us need present no insuperable obstacle to our really loving him—loving Jesus himself, the concrete person who, only through his seeming disappearance into the incomprehensibility of God, can come right up close to us as the concrete, historical person he is—on condition that we *want* to love him, that we have the courage to throw our arms around him.

There are still two observations to be made about this loving relationship of ours to Jesus. First, the experience of true love for "third parties" is in no way constricted or diminished by our love for Jesus. This "ordinary love for neighbor" is precisely a prerequisite of our love for Jesus. Here we may safely paraphrase what we read in John: How can we love Jesus, whom we cannot see, if we do not love our neighbor whom we do see? And the other way about: This love for neighbor can and should actually grow through a love for Jesus, for it is only in a loving relationship with Jesus that we conceive the possibilities of love for neighbor that otherwise we should simply not hold to be feasible, but which present themselves nonetheless wherever we subsume our neighbor in our love for Jesus because he or she is Jesus' brother or sister. Further: It happens that this immediate love for Jesus, as it is meant in these pages, is not simply present from the start. It must grow and ripen. The tender interiority of this love, to which it need not be afraid to admit, is the fruit of patience, prayer, and an ever renewed immersion in Scripture. It is the gift of God's Spirit. We cannot commandeer it, we cannot seize it violently and without discretion. But we may always know that the very aspiration to such love is already its beginning, and that we have a promise of its fulfillment.

2 · Our Relationship to Jesus

The Modernizing of Christology

We have arrived at a point where we must at last describe the relationship between Jesus and ourselves more precisely and with some degree of clarity. From the very nature of the case, this relationship can be described in either of two ways. We may simply begin with Jesus and try to say who he is, in the sense of who he is believed and accepted to be, and then add that it is just this acceptance of Jesus, thus known of, believed in, and understood, that we mean by our "relationship" to him. Or we can attack the question quite the other way about, and actually seek to describe this relationship, beginning with ourselves, and then say: What the particularity of our relationship to Jesus yields concerning Jesus himself, the understanding of him that is implied in this relationship, is indeed what he is in reality. In either case it is ultimately a matter of our saying who he is in our understanding. But as we have said, we can try to do it beginning with him, or beginning with ourselves.

Evidently these two approaches will not be unequivocally distinguishable from each other, let alone separable. A given relationship to Jesus is also a practical condition for recognizing him "objectively" in his particularity. And, vice versa, a proposition of this kind about Jesus himself cannot emerge exclusively from the expression of how we relate to him ourselves. After all, this is always the case: Love and the beloved condition each other mutually, and the description of one implies a proposition about the other.

Let us begin our attempt with the first approach. We are en-

25

deavoring to say more precisely who this Jesus is whom we love—
with whom we seek to have this altogether unique relationship. In
this first approach we presuppose basically everything that a normal Catholic Christology is able to say about Jesus. Obviously,
only an extremely imperfect, sketchy, and fragmentary synopsis,
or "modernization," if you will, of this Christology can be undertaken in a few pages. On the one hand, it is evident that all such
Christology, as lived in the Church, derives ultimately from Jesus'
witness to himself—from the manner in which he himself understood his task and mission, his cross, and, in these, himself. We
could very well begin our investigation into this self-understanding of Jesus with the witness of the New Testament, and ask what
Jesus himself says there of himself and his task. We may ask what
can be acknowledged as unconditionally valid historically in this
historical witness of the New Testament—without fear of any ac-
cretions that would effectively falsify the self-understanding of
Jesus that this historical account purports to represent. But we
may also rely on the Christians of these many centuries since, on
the history of their faith and on the courage of that faith—in a
word, on the faith-consciousness of the Church—and begin with
the Church's faith-interpretation of Jesus' self-understanding.

This faith-understanding of the Church, and of the history of
the Church, can be examined historically for its credibility. In so
examining it, however, one should not underestimate the significance and force of this faith of the Christian centuries in itself. In
religious matters one should not be too quick to wish to be more
clever than the numberless human beings of centuries past with
their faith in Jesus. People who have come later do not really show
themselves to be wiser and more clever in their veneration of individuals than those who came earlier. In other cases, with Mao, for
instance, splendor and veneration have faded away very quickly
for someone who once commanded all but the adoration of count-
less millions of human beings. Thus the vitality of faith in Jesus
down through two millenia is itself a consideration for faith today.

The Messiah: God Become a Human Being

Clearly we shall not have space here to offer a precise and thor-
oughgoing presentation of the "historical Jesus" as the Christ in

the proper sense of the expression, either in the first or in the second of our possible ways of approach to our relationship to Jesus. Nor shall we make any attempt to keep all the various routes that are actually taken in describing this relationship (his own interpretation of himself, the actual faith of the Church, and so on) distinct from one another. Finally, it is indisputable here that these various approaches to Jesus, where our faith and its legitimation are concerned, are always grounded in the credibility of his resurrection as God's seal on his self-understanding. This faith in the resurrection requires a justification of its own, of course. The unity (not the identity) of matter and spirit, the hope of one's own "resurrection" (correctly understood), the witness of Jesus' disciples, and other things as well must all be kept in mind. All this is simply presupposed in the considerations which follow.

Under these presuppositions, then, perhaps we can say (while granting, of course, the equal legitimacy of other formulations and approaches): Jesus understands himself as the Messiah. He is convinced that with himself the definitive, unsurpassable Kingdom of God has arrived—that in him God shares himself and communicates his own glory and excellence, consoling a sinful world with his irrevocable pardon, speaking his last, definitive Word, after which there shall be no other—and that this Word is indeed God himself, in his own excellence. It will not be of interest to us here whether and to what extent Jesus himself employed the word "Messiah," which of course already had an accepted content. In any case it was used by his disciples as an expression of his correct understanding of himself: otherwise they would not have called him "the Christ." One can express the concept of "Messiah" in completely different ways, from entirely different points of view. But in every case the Messiah is the person with and through whom the definitive Kingdom of God has come. And ultimately, if we may be permitted something of a metaphysical observation here, this Kingdom of God is simply God himself, and not something distinct from him.

Now, if the Messiah is the definitive and irrevocable *self*-affirmation of God, then we already have, it seems to me, what traditional Christology seeks to express in the concept of Jesus' divine sonship, the concept of the hypostatic union, the incarnation of the eternal Son of God, and so on. Whether this position of mine is correct or not is, to be sure, open to discussion. It could perhaps be objected that the concept of Messiah, even as we have just described it, and the concept of God become a human being are not identical. But I think that these two concepts *are* entirely identifiable with each other, provided we clearly understand that "Messiah" means substantially more than just any sort of prophet sent by God —that "Messiah" means the vehicle and bearer of a definitive message that can basically no longer be transcended, a message in which God definitively "commits himself."

A like identification of these two concepts, let us note in passing, would enjoy the apologetical advantage of enabling one to show an immediate connection between the conception of Jesus in the older parts of the New Testament and the christological faith of the Church's magisterium. Anyone holding that the concept of Messiah is lower in content, signifies less, than the concept of the eternal Son of God will have to solve the difficulty of why, in the New Testament, Jesus stresses the Messianic concept in expressing his self-understanding even more than that of the incarnate Word. But if we identify these two concepts in their proper signification, this difficulty disappears.

A God Who Gives Himself

How is it that we can identify these two concepts—that of "Messiah" and that of "incarnate Word and Son of God"? Let us consider this question, just very briefly, in the following terms. When God utters himself in a merely created reality, then this reality will express him indeed—but, as something merely created, as something finite, something that (because it is finite) leaves room for something alongside it or following it. It will necessarily be something merely provisional. Hence, in my view, the proposition follows: Any reality in the history of the world that, as God's creature, is simply finite, will in no wise be able to make any definitive, unsurpassable, irrevocable proclamation. If God wishes to say something that is no longer merely provisional in the world, something definitive and irrevocable, not simply in words, of course, but through reality and deeds, then this reality will have to have such an association with God as to be the reality of God himself. Of course it will not be simply identical with him (for then the infinite God would not be changeless and eternal in himself), but it will have to be bound up and become one with him in such a way that, were this reality indeed to be surpassed by another reality, God himself would have to change. Or conversely: If God wishes to bestow his definitive, irrevocable self-affirmation on the world, then this manifestation, this utterance, must be bound up with him in a real oneness in such a way that, were it to be surpassed, God himself would cease to be himself. Something really irrevocable and definitive can only be in the world if it has a unity with God himself in which God himself, as himself, is "engaged."

Ordinary religious prophets, religiously creative human beings, have basically always lived with the awareness that they can be surpassed—an awareness that, in view of God's infinite plenitude of being and infinite capacities, such a prophet simply *cannot* "say the last word." Of course they are right in this. Indeed this is true precisely when and to the extent that their message is genuine. We may admit that such a prophet says a word that is inspired by God. But a last, final, unsurpassable word vis-à-vis God's infinite fullness of reality, vis-à-vis the boundlessness of his possibilities, is manifestly and in principle impossible. When one is dealing precisely with God, either what is definitive is God himself or there can be nothing definitive. Were there indeed to be a reality in the world that is unsurpassable, then this reality, unlike any other created thing, must belong to the holy God himself as his own reality, and he must in this reality, created indeed but belonging to himself, vouchsafe himself to the world as inmost gift, in his own actual divine excellence.

I should say that, except in Jesus, this has not only never occurred but has never even been claimed. Jesus is the only prophet who claims (and at the same time does not render himself religiously impossible) to be the last, unsurpassable, definitive word in the history that transpires between God and the world. He likewise makes the claim that this last, definitive word is actually God's genuine *self*-assertion, in which God bestows not something created by him, be it ever so excellent, but actually bestows himself. One can consider such a statement very metaphysical and abstract, but it is basically what we have in Jesus' appearance among us. God himself comes and saves us; and this redemption—as the New Testament teaches, especially in Paul and John—is not the reorientation and consummation of a finite world, just in itself, but God himself, God giving himself. This is the content of the messianic message, the content of God's self-communication as irrevocably given in Jesus.

To be sure, God is always and everywhere dealing with human beings, in the history of the individual as in that of the collective mass of humanity, especially in the Old Testament. But all these encounters were only "trial runs," though of course they may have been buoyed up by the secret, wild hope that they could *herald* a definitive, blessed nearness to God himself. These encounters never dared the *certain* hope that they could never be revoked. The "new and everlasting covenant" was hoped for in the Old Testament, but it was not present—not present as a historical, tangible, irrevocable covenant. But it is present in Jesus.

Then the tangible human reality of Jesus must be the reality of God himself. Not that Jesus is no longer finite and human—not that he disappears, as it were, into the incomprehensibility and intangibility of God—but this reality of Jesus as created reality must have another relationship to God than is otherwise given in the world. As his history shows, Jesus has an altogether genuine creaturely relationship to God. He prayed, he struggled with God's will, he had genuine human experiences, even religious experiences, and so on. But it was in just this whole human reality that God *himself* could be genuinely present, and it is thus that God bestows *himself* upon the world in the history of this human being, including of course his death and resurrection, in irrevocable self-commitment.

Problems of a Traditional Christology

Traditional Christology seeks to express this unique, singular relationship between God and the reality of Jesus, in which Jesus becomes the unsurpassable, definitive Word of God in the world, in the concept of the "hypostatic union." It seeks to render this hypostatic union understandable by what is called the *communicatio idiomatum*, or exchange of concrete attributes. The doctrine of the *communicatio idiomatum* states that there obtains between

God's eternal Word and the human reality of Jesus a unity (which does not mean an identity) such that the attributes of Jesus' human reality can be predicated of the eternal Word—the Word has become a human being, the eternal Word has suffered, the Son of the Father died, and so on. And, vice versa, wherever Jesus' human reality is grasped in its definitive concretion, in which it may by no means be thought of as existing in separation from God, divine attributes can be predicated of Jesus—Jesus is God, and so on. This doctrine of the communication of attributes does indeed force upon us the unity between the eternal Word of God and the human reality of Jesus as a unique and concrete reality, and that is where its truth lies. A Catholic Christology can scarcely do without the communication of attributes. But, like all human expressions, it has its difficulties. De facto, Christians who start with the *communicatio idiomatum* are led, over and over again, to think of an *identity*, a plain and simple sameness, between divinity and humanity in Jesus, instead of thinking of the *unity* between God and the human reality of Jesus. Naturally, a Christian cannot long hold this error, inconsistent as it is with his or her authentic beliefs —otherwise the human reality of Jesus would disappear altogether. But the misunderstanding that can accompany the communication of idioms, contrary to its proper intent, all too often has the effect of persuading us that Jesus, or what we call Jesus, is a kind of uniform worn by the eternal Word of God, and the real distinction (not disconnection!) between divinity and humanity in Jesus Christ is overlooked.

If you ask an ordinary, average Christian, "Can you really think that the eternal Son of God, Jesus Christ, can pray to the Father? Is he someone who can be faced with the inscrutability of the will of God? Is he someone who can have experiences, not only with respect to earthly things, but with respect to God's intentions as well? Can you really think of him as of someone humble and obedient? Can he perhaps actually learn obedience, as we read in the letter to the Hebrews?"—if we ask an ordinary Christian these things, he or she will at least be tempted to say that all of this is impossible—for, "after all, Jesus is God." Thus we are forced to conclude that the *communicatio idiomatum*, indispensable as it may be, has its difficulties as well.

The Dogmas of Unity and Distinction

One way of reducing the complex of problems associated with the *communicatio idiomatum* to an abstract common denominator would be the following. The *communicatio idiomatum* is expressed via an "is," or at least the word "is" is used in expressing it. Jesus "is" God, Jesus "is" a human being. Now, in ordinary human parlance, this "is" occurs where there is a substantial reality to be expressed of a subject and a predicate in a proposition of *identity*. "Peter is a human being" is a proposition designating the concrete identity between being a human being and being Peter. But this identity is not what is asserted in the "is"-expressions of the communication of idioms, nor indeed is this the actual intent of orthodox Christology. Rather, what is meant and expressed is a unique manner of *unity*, a oneness obtaining here that occurs nowhere else.

But the communication of attributes not only expresses this unity (which is not identity), it not only makes it understandable, it also *obscures* it. It obscures it because the "is" with which the communication of attributes is expressed predicates, in other cases, an identity, and not a simple unity—for this manner of unity occurs nowhere else.

All of this is the subject of the unequivocal teaching of the Council of Chalcedon, and hence is a truth of faith. It is not merely an opinion which a Christian who wishes to hold it, and who happens to like to think somewhat more rationally, may hold as a matter of option. It is a truth which a Christian basically *must* hold, and hold as revealed. In other words, it is not just that we have a dogma of a unique unity between godhood and humanity in Jesus, it is equally a dogma that this unity does not mean sameness—that godhood and humanity in this Jesus Christ are present "unconfused," unmingled, although indeed undivided from each other. And this dogma of a distinction between the two natures must be kept just as much in view if a Christian seeks to speak correctly of Jesus Christ, in conformity with the faith, as the dogma of the undividedness of divinity and humanity in Jesus Christ.

Consequently, it is also clear that when we speak of "one person" in Jesus Christ, and say that this "person," for the christological faith of the Church, is the person of the eternal Word of

God, we are not depriving the human Jesus, with respect to his humanity, of those realities meant and expressed in our modern, current word "person." "Person," for us today, means the subjective center of the activities of awareness and freedom. In this sense there is of course also a *human*, finite, creaturely personality in Jesus Christ—a subjective, self-aware center of activity that behaves in freedom, and which evidently and necessarily belongs to what the ancient Church called human "nature," as does everything else essentially human. If we forget this, we do homage in our own day to what the history of dogma calls Apollinarianism—an ancient heresy which held that the actual human, created soul in Jesus Christ is replaced by the divine Word, so that Jesus has no creaturely, subjective center of human acts: He has the divine Word in its place.

Such of course is not the case. Jesus can pray, Jesus can be humble, Jesus can fall mute before the incomprehensibility of God, Jesus can be obedient, Jesus can have new experiences. Jesus confronts his history *as a human being*, and not as someone who could, as it were, look at his whole life story and say, "I always know everything in advance." The altogether human reality and history of Jesus is not just the material through which a divine "I," God himself, manifests himself, as a puppet on a string might be manipulated by the person really performing the action. Obviously, this subjective human personality in reality has a relationship to God as fully active as that of any other human being, and *thus* (without being diminished thereby) belongs to God as God's own reality. The radical oneness of this human reality (along with its subjectivity) with the divine reality of the eternal Word, far from diminishing this subjectivity of the human being, Jesus, actually enhances and radicalizes it. For the nearer one is to God, the more one is a human being, in all human freedom.

Tolerance for Modern Christologies

By way of supplemental reflection on the foregoing, I should like to make just a few theological observations here, which the reader without great interest in theological controversies may simply skip over. For others I hope they may be of some modest profit, however little they may be intended to offer anything actually very new.

One ought not assume the concept of the hypostatic union to be a plain and simple notion in every respect, so that the only question would be whether one accepts or rejects it. It is not as easy as all that. If we were ever to leave off asking what is meant by it, if we were to fail to recognize our right and duty to make ever new attempts to say what is meant by it and therefore necessarily to employ new concepts and formulations, we would be turning acceptance of the dogma of the hypostatic union into a proposition which has no further interest than whether or not it enjoys the formal approbation of the Church.

But how does one clarify what is really meant by the unity expressed in this dogma? After all, there are many kinds of "unity" among realities other than that of simple identity. Hence one must state *what* unity, or oneness, is meant here. I suspect that the reason not a few people (theologians included) seem to think that this unity scarcely stands in need of further explanation is that they see this unity, perhaps not altogether clearly and explicitly, as given through the Word as vehicle of the existence of Jesus' human reality—that the Word brings this human reality about through itself.

But even apart from the fact that most theologians today appear to ascribe a created "existence" to the human reality of Jesus, this interpretation of the unity between Word and human reality in Jesus is at most a nonbinding "theologoumenon," which anyone who wishes to do so is permitted to reject. This conceptualization is thus not a clarification of the meaning of the dogma itself within its own framework. Nor are conceptualizations of unity that are unconsciously limited to unities observed in the world of our experience (unity of body and soul, pieces of material connected together, and so on) of any help. In fact, they threaten the true sense of the hypostatic union. It would appear, then, that the only viable explanation is the one the hypostatic union seeks to give through the *communicatio idiomatum*: This substantial unity is such that it is the vehicle of the *communicatio idiomatum* ontologically. I hold this manner of explanation to be legitimate and indispensable. Nevertheless, it must be conceded that the *communicatio idiomatum* itself simply cannot be understood as easily as may first appear. For when we predicate the particularity of a "nature" in Jesus of the "person" as being really attributable to it *in quantum,* "in so far as," this one and the same person is denominated from the other nature (which, after all, is what is meant by the *communicatio idiomatum*)—then the question still remains what exactly is meant by this "in so far as," what it means ontologically. Were we to respond that in this case it would be better not to say "in so far as," but simply "who" (for instance, "the person of Jesus, *who*—also—is God, has died"), we would have the same question all over again: What is the exact ontological meaning of this "is also"? The question of the character and quality of this unity is thus with us once more. In other words, if this "is," the "communication" of attributes, this hypostatic unity, indeed denotes no identity, then what does it denote, and what does it surely not denote, if the Chalcedonian *asynchytōs,* "without confusion," "without commingling," is to be saved?

Those who spurn the explanations of Schillebeeckx, Küng, and Schoonenberg as unsatisfactory may be in the right. We shall indulge in no adjudications here. However, they should be asked to suggest better orthodox formulations than the ones they reject, for we simply are unable to say that this unique union of divinity and humanity obtaining in Jesus is being favored with an adequately clear and understandable explanation today.

Let it not be interjected here that we are after all dealing with a basic mystery of Christianity, which is to be worshiped but not thought on any further. We may not be allowed to dispense with the mystery—surely not. But are we thereby excused from thinking about it? Have we no more obligation to avoid misunderstandings of it? If we really cannot say that the concept of the hypostatic union is a self-evident concept of everyday life, then it *must* be explained, and we must reckon with the fact that, in this attempt to explain it, new questions and demands for clarification will appear. One cannot say that the history of Christology—for Christology indisputably has a history—has simply come to an end today merely because nothing further occurs to certain theologians.

But if this history is to continue, new formulations have to be attempted. And the attempts must of course be subjected to testing and measurement by the standards of Scripture and the definitions of the Councils, as well as of the whole faith-understanding of the Church. But they must also measure up to the criterion of whether they are genuinely serviceable for the faith-understanding of a human being of today, who has his or her modern horizons of comprehension. It is not an a priori evidence that, just because one theologian or another has the impression that a new formulation fails to subsume and account for the old, binding christological truth, his or her impression is necessarily correct. (Pius X had the impression that the Yahwist hypothesis was irreconcilable with the obligatory teaching of the Church. John Paul II no longer has this impression.) If someone is of the conviction that, for instance, the unity between two persons who love one another is a more real unity, a oneness charged with more reality, than the unity between a table top and a table leg, or than the unity of two molecules in the oneness of a loaf of bread (which Trent thinks of as a single substance), we cannot a priori prevent this person from describing the oneness in Christ in "psychological" or "moral" categories (provided he or she does not permit the uniqueness and incommensurability of this oneness to escape from view), and hence to be of the opinion that he or she has expressed this unique unity more radically in these categories than in attempting to express it in more "ontological" concepts—which, after all, however unintentionally, borrow from observable physical models.

Here, of course, a further question arises, one which we cannot take the space to investigate here: whether formulations of this unity proceeding from existential points of departure like the above are, after all, actually acceptable, or on the contrary may be legitimately suppressed in virtue of a certain principle of semantic discipline in the Church. The very scarcity of theologians who hold these new formulations to be correct may constitute an argument, not that the new formulations are necessarily untrue, but that they ought to be avoided just because their points of departure are inaccessible to the majority of Christians in the Church—of which the number of theologians rejecting these formulations is, once again, an indication.

However this may be, considerations of this kind, as we have barely suggested here, would once more legitimate a greater reciprocal tolerance in the Church than actually prevails. After all, history shows that much of what was once rejected as false doctrine—the real Nestorius, perhaps Pelagius, the Reformers' teaching on justification, theories of the origin of the Old Testament, and so on—were later judged with much more leniency, and on good grounds indeed, which the other side also acknowledged. Could we not permit such flexibility of thinking and critique to prevail before the fact?

In Jesus, God Has Come Absolutely Close to Me

Of course, we may find all this quite complicated and difficult, and we may doubt whether one really need occupy oneself with all these hard questions and propositions in order to be a true Christian. Conversely, we might extract from everything that has been presented here so far the following: If I am really convinced that in Jesus God has personally bestowed himself upon me (and has done so in an unsurpassable way, such as exists nowhere else)— and I think any Christian can understand this relatively easily and act in conformity with it—then I have really embraced and covered the whole of Christology in this simple, modest notion. But it is precisely this unpretentious understanding—that in Jesus God has personally bestowed himself on me definitively and unsurpassably—which the faith-consciousness of the Church can and must reflect upon, develop, clarify in further formulations, and remove from primitivizing and reductive misunderstandings. Naturally, then, the whole long history of the development of dogma, from the synoptics through Paul and John to the Councils of the ancient Church, was an altogether correct, necessary, and indispensable history. Indeed, we could even say that it would be well for this history to continue today in a more clearly expressed way, in a more courageous and unbiased way, than is actually the case. It might be well for the Church, precisely out of fidelity to its pristine dogma, to seek more boldly to say in a new form just what is meant by that dogma. Perhaps it would be well for the Church not to rest content with merely handing on its correct, abiding christological truths—confined as these necessarily are in finite, human propositions—in too rigid and ossified a form. The old Christology remains our Christology, to be sure. But we have the right and the duty to think that Christology through over and over again, the right and the duty really to assimilate it, and, where difficulties of understanding arise, to attempt to say what is actually meant in, perhaps, a different way. We have the right and duty to consider things from another approach.

There can be no doubt that other approaches are possible. There would be possibilities for formulating our Christology (the old meaning in new words) from a point of departure in a modern existential ontology, provided this ontology itself is correctly understood. We could perhaps formulate the authentic christological datum anew in an evolutionary worldview, in the style of Teilhard de Chardin, and see Christ Jesus as the Omega point bringing about cosmic evolution from a moment of operation in the future, but already active in the world and its development. We could perhaps formulate the old Christology as a correctly understood and cautiously formulated divine drama of God-in-process, expressing it in a theology of the history of God (understood in a Christian sense, and without compromising the dogma of God's eternal immutability). We could go on to cite other possibilities. But the simple, unassuming Christian, working out his or her own salvation in humility and hope, can and must say: In Jesus, God himself, personally, has come absolutely close to me, and has done something in the history of humanity that can never be canceled. For he cannot cancel himself—and he has "done himself" in Jesus. And in this coming-near of God himself in Jesus, this God says to me: I am here as your own, definitive, irrevocable, liberating, forgiving glory, still present in history, which it is for you to bring to accomplishment. For myself, what is definitive about my love is already present in history—in your life. Why? Because Jesus lives and abides forever.

What Happens When We Love Jesus?

Now let us consider our relationship to Jesus from the other pole of this relationship: from the side of the human being who, through his or her love, fashions a unity, a oneness, with Jesus. To be sure, a like relationship of the human being to Jesus has as its vehicle what we call the divine, or supernatural, virtue of love. Clearly, when we take on this loving relationship to Jesus, it is basically not we who seize the initiative, for we are ever but the respondents to this love, those who answer—those to whom God's love has come in advance, whom it has "prevented," anticipated. It is God's love which makes our love possible at all. Theologically speaking, the radical character of love for Jesus Christ is made possible only by the anticipating force of Love itself, which Love is always available to our freedom and is ultimately God himself. God loves us, and this love is a reality in which he personally communicates and shares himself with the inmost center of our being, and *hence* we can love Jesus.

But all of this being presupposed, it is still possible and needful to describe love for Jesus with a greater measure of exactitude, and thereby once again to make it more clearly understandable what it is we seize on as his reality when we believe in Jesus himself. We keep in mind, of course, that both of these ways of meditation, from Jesus to us and from our love for Jesus to him, always condition each other reciprocally, so that a description of this love of ours for Jesus will always coexpress the other vantage. This goes without saying, and does not imply any disparagement of this second way of considering things.

We love Jesus. We have already considered how this is radically possible, how we can thus move out beyond the confines of space and time to which human beings are subject. The ultimate and really telling proof of this possibility, of course, is that there really is such love—that there are people who actually do make Jesus the center of their thinking and willing, their love, their whole existence. *Ab esse ad posse valet illatio*—actuality demonstrates possibility—here as elsewhere, and any problems arising out of this possibility are counterbalanced, however difficult the possibility may be to analyze, by the consideration that there must be this possibility since the actuality exists.

Then what actually occurs when we love Jesus?

Unconditional and Definitive

We may begin with the unhesitating assertion that in loving Jesus we love an actual human being, a real person. We seek him, we think about him, we speak with him, we feel his nearness, we have the perception, the sensation, that our own life is very substantially co-formed through him, through this other, through his own thinking and feeling and perception, through his life and lot, and so on. However we love anyone, so at all events is our love for Jesus. There remains, then—since we need not describe genuine, personal love between two persons in general in any greater detail here—only the question of what particularity, what uniqueness and radical character, this genuinely human love for Jesus has, precisely in respect of Jesus, as contradistinguished from love for other persons.

We could of course attempt to answer this question from a great variety of starting points. But let us begin with the fact that human love generally, however unconditional, radical, and definitive it might *like* to be, is still codetermined in some way by a secret reservation. The lover's fear of "not measuring up" to the beloved, of not doing justice to him or her—or that the beloved could deny the lover a requital of love, which the latter requires in order to continue in this love—the terrible fear of loving someone and having it emerge that there is no longer anything about this person to make him or her lovable—the inward threat of love's unreservedness, arising from the fact that we may simply not *allow* love to be as unconditional as we could wish it—the question of how far this love, which seeks to be unconditional, really reaches, whether it is not after all really only a transitory infatuation, gradually dying, after all, and killed by time—these and similar reservations or fears, avowedly or not, are tacitly or expressly bound up with one person's human love for another. It could scarcely be otherwise—indeed, if such earthly love, out of the will to unconditionality and definitiveness, were to seek to deny this inner sense of threat, it would be basically denying its own nature. It would be inauthentic. It would be ascribing to the lover, and even more to the beloved, an unconditionality and absolute validity which is simply not attributable to them. It would be feigning a certainty and security which it simply does not possess in reality, and it would end by anxiously overstraining its limits through this self-deception.

And yet, in spite of all—despite the "threatenedness" of this love, despite the circumstance that it actually cannot ultimately stand surety for itself—it is still a love that reaches for unconditionality, for definitiveness, for real, radical self-surrender. We cannot and need not undertake a consideration here of how this inner dilemma of human love is overcome—how it comes about that even in human love, as it factually occurs in the everyday, there can be the calm certainty that this love abides, that it is definitive, and that it does actually realize and fulfill its ultimate nature. Our purpose in presenting its fears and difficulties here is to see by contrast what love for Jesus means. Here a *definitive* love is said to occur and seeks to occur. The last reservations and insecurities of all human love are transcended in the case of love for Jesus, and love can be really unconditional, unconditional in the last extreme and in all dimensions. It can, and it actually is. It may rightfully ascribe to itself an unconditionality, a definitiveness—the right of extravagance, of boundlessness and unreserve. For in Jesus it knows the Ground of this unconditionality to be given in indissoluble conjunction with him: the God of faithfulness, his *own* unconditionality. To be sure, in our own life this love for Jesus is always only just getting under way. It is never completed and fulfilled. It must grow, it must learn. It must conquer and occupy all the human being's different dimensions. But at bottom this love for Jesus is unconditional and of an inner absoluteness that "fills out," completes, a human being altogether, and truly makes him or her over to Jesus as the uniquely loved human being.

A Love of Total Surrender

None of this needs closer description for our purposes. Instead, let us turn at once to the question of the prerequisites for a love like this—what this love must have in order to be able to be earnestly conceived and actually to exist in the first place. And let us consider not just the prerequisites in the person loving Jesus but those in Jesus, too—in the person who is to be loved in this fashion. Here we must assuredly say that, where the person loving is concerned, such love can only occur when its vehicle is the power of the unconditionality of God himself. This is what scholastic theology means with its formulation that this salvific love for Jesus occurs by the power and as the consummation of the infused supernatural virtue of divine faith, in which God, through his prevenient grace, is himself principle, guarantor, and vessel of this love of a human being for God. Love for Jesus Christ has an unconditionality that is precisely the unconditionality of the love of a human being for God, and it therefore requires the same divine grace as is necessary for this love of a human being for God, in which the human being surrenders to God in a final, most radical way, makes himself or herself over to him, and as if in an ecstatic bursting forth from self, never more permits the human being to return to self.

But in the matter at hand, the important question is what conditions this love requires in Jesus, in order for it really to be this radical, unconditional, self-assured love which cannot be deceived, and which is what we require of our love for Jesus. It is precisely here, then, that we must say that a human being can and may be loved in this way, without any reserve, only when this human being enjoys an absolute and definitive union with God.

The force and unconditionality of human love is often expressed in the notion that the lover is willing to share everything with the beloved unconditionally—to identify with the beloved's lot whatever that lot may be, even to being ready to go into the utter darkness and damnation of hell with the beloved. If we read these utterances as the passionate and emotional expression of a legitimate unconditionality of human love, they may of course be allowed their validity. But in all realism, we can and must say: The only one who can be loved with an absolutely selfless and unconditional love, to the last extreme, to the surrender of the last fiber of one's existence, will be the one who possesses that purity, that clarity, that unconditionality, that absolute security and reliability, which is only to be found where the beloved is so associated and united with the unconditionality, purity, clarity, and boundlessness of God that all these divine characteristics can in some sense be asserted of the beloved, be it only by participation. Every lover tells the beloved, "I love you unconditionally." But once more, if this love is not to be perverted by this very unconditionality, this unconditionality must precisely include a reservation, since no one is permitted to dare to wish to go to hell with another. Such a wish would destroy the basis of this love—destroy it in its very roots.

The only other possibility is for this unconditional love to know that the human being who is to be loved with unconditionality is unconditionally accepted by God. But this is known by one human being of another in this world only of Jesus of Nazareth (or, by derivation, of those who securely belong to him, who are included in his affirmation).

Jesus Loved Anonymously

With a view to some measure of clarification and conquest of a difficulty that arises here, we must make certain further observations along the present lines. The following objection, after all, could be raised: Suppose some person, wherever he or she might be, to be in fact indissolubly united to God and, in virtue of an absolute predestination, to remain so. This person could then be loved with the unconditional love that we appear to reserve for Jesus alone. We have only to think of Mary. Such an unconditional love can, then, it would seem, rest on other grounds than we have required in Jesus in the hypostatic union. The argument we have brought forward would now seem to be unsound, positing as it does an utterly radical attachment of the beloved to God as the basis of the unconditionality of love for him or her. What answer is to be made to this objection?

To be sure, the definitiveness of a human being's union with God opens the way for a true definitiveness of love for him or her (even where one's love for someone else may be greater on other grounds). But on what does the definitiveness of the union with God which forms the basis of such love *rest?* It rests on God's love-creating condescension. But this love-creating condescension has become unequivocally accessible and irreversible in the salvation history of the world only in Jesus. For it is only when God has affirmed and bestowed his concrete love (not in a theorem) on the world in the form of a love that is irreversible from his side that the unconditional reliability and utter self-assurance of a love for a human being is possible. But this affirmation and bestowal is available only in Jesus.

To put it theologically: A mutual association and union of a human being and God short of hypostatic union "engages" God himself only conditionally and provisionally. Where, then, one loves a human being as someone in radical union with God, either the reservation prevails of which we have already spoken, or the love will be absolute indeed, and legitimately so, but will exist under the condition—the tacit condition—that God has indeed embraced and assumed this loved person in the absolute affirmation he has bestowed upon Jesus (and upon him alone), and that it may indeed be taken as a certainty that this person is embraced and assumed in this affirmation (something we cannot know with utter certainty in this life). Thus the unconditionality of human love can be experienced indeed and is altogether a praiseworthy thing, but the Christian knows that it rests, at least "anonymously," on the unconditionality of God's affirmation of love for human beings, which has become absolute and irrevocable only in Jesus.

Perhaps one can and should say all this still more cautiously, exactly, and precisely. This can be done quite briefly and simply: Where love can really abandon all reservations, definitively and with absolute assurance, where love can really live out to the last its most proper, most original nature as unconditional self-giving and surrender to the other, there Jesus as such is "co-loved" as the Ground of this love—even where that blessed Name is as yet altogether unknown to the one who loves. But we Christians can name this primordially and radically loved person. We call him Jesus of Nazareth. And when one really knows what takes place in a love like this—when one knows the prerequisites for such a love in the beloved if that love is not to be the most enormous perversion or ultimate absurdity of existence—one sees that the prerequisites and conditions for such a love in the beloved include everything basically posited in what the Christian faith confesses of Jesus of Nazareth, as the one who exists in a union with God that is absolute and of a substantial order. As we have said, this explanation, which is based on this special sort of correspondence between love for Jesus and the reality of Jesus as expressed in Christian Christology, could and should now perhaps be examined in closer detail. And yet we must rest content with what has been said.

Sinking into the Incomprehensibility of God

There is one thing, however, that we may not be allowed to omit. In this love for Jesus, this love of an unconditional and radically unique kind, what occurs is not the completion or fulfillment of the human being in the order of things human. What occurs is precisely that unconditional and radical act of human existence, ultimate and unique, in which the human being surrenders to *God*, accepting his eternal brilliance and radically mysterious incomprehensibility. One who loves Jesus loves someone whose destiny he or she seeks to share in this love; and precisely because he or she does so, he or she surrenders himself or herself to Jesus' destiny of death. He or she is prepared to commit everything with the dying Lord to the incomprehensibility of God—the whole world and the self—quietly, unconditionally, even if this God seems darker than the absurdity upon which the philosophy of a Sartre or a Camus is centered. Of course, this Christian act of surrender to God with Jesus is not the event of pure absurdity that the will to damnation is (if indeed this will ever factually exists, which is to be feared but ultimately cannot be known), but rather is still illuminated by a final, secret light, humbly received as Jesus received it in his abandonment when he said "Father."

Thus the absolute, the utterly unconditional, can only occur, when it occurs in the human being at all, in the surrender of everything to the incomprehensibility of God. For whatever is not identical with God, taken by itself alone, is finite, conditional, and capable of being replaced or expelled by something else. It can be loved, yes, but it can also be denied love, because, precisely, it is finite. Thus the final unconditionality and absolute radicality of human existence can only transpire when one allows oneself to sink away into the incomprehensibility of God; and the assertion that one loves Jesus definitively and unconditionally, in an utterly unique way, is in no way a contradiction of this. Indeed Jesus himself, as the Crucified One who rose again, is, on the one hand, the human being who has accomplished this unconditional capitulation to God; and on the other hand, it is in his case alone that we know with the certitude of faith that this capitulation and self-surrender has actually been accepted—that the whole of the existence of this person has been given over to God without stint or reserve and that God has accepted and taken up that surrender and that existence.

All of this comes with faith in Jesus as the Resurrected One. Unconditional love for Jesus, which will in no wise be possible and forthcoming elsewhere than precisely in the case of Jesus—and the unconditional self-surrender of the human being to God, which alone can constitute the absoluteness of human existence—are, at bottom, one. For this Jesus is the Crucified One, the one who sank into death, into the incomprehensibility of God, and who in this fact and deed is the blessedly Accepted One. The absoluteness of Christianity is God, and the absoluteness of the surrender of human existence to God means, when all is said and done, Jesus of Nazareth. And both are one, in what we call in scholastic Christology the hypostatic union of the eternal Word with the human reality of Jesus.

PART II

Jesus Christ as the Meaning of Life

"Meaning," nowadays, is a kind of key word in philosophical and religious reflection and discourse. If love for Jesus is not just some sort of harmless feeling that someone happens to have while someone else happens not to, but the salvific intervention of God in our lives, then in order to give a better answer to the question of love for Jesus, it will be helpful to restate it in the form of the question whether and in what sense Jesus Christ is the meaning of our life. This restatement will then possibly provide us with further clarification as to what it means to love Jesus.

The subject is sufficiently general that it actually takes in the whole Christian faith. We are dealing with a topic of measureless proportions, then, and we can only say a limited amount about it —indeed, only fragmentarily, and inevitably by making a somewhat arbitrary selection of material, and so orienting our responses to the central question of the meaning of Jesus for our lives. Much of what is meaningful, and what could and should be said about this subject, must, perhaps to the reader's chagrin, remain unsaid.

To be sure, we shall seek to respond to our question from a point of departure in the whole of the normal, orthodox Christian faith. In doing so, however, we shall inevitably be packaging our material in an unmistakably individual and therefore somewhat subjective theology that is not binding in faith. Where this comes expressly to the writer's consciousness, naturally he will refer to it. But in thus packaging our material in an individual theology (in our language, in the emphasis on certain propositions of the Christian faith, in our selection of statements of Christian truth and the manner of connecting them, and so on) it can occur that the writer himself may simply not notice that this is a package, or else, in the interests of brevity, does not call explicit attention to it.

Perhaps too, our considerations in the following pages may emerge as somewhat disappointing to some when it is seen that they will not so much intone a triumphal hymn to the Christian response to the question of life's meaning, as they will be an attempt to indicate the limits of even the Christian answer to the question of life's meaning. For, when all is said and done, all one can do is invite the human being to commit his or her endless striving for some kind of fulfilling meaning to the intangible mystery of God, in the resolute determination of a faith that knows how to hope, and to be willing to enter into the divine darkness as the solitary dawning of the true Light.

Finally, a Christian answer to the question of the global meaning of human existence must keep in mind right from the start that a global answer will not spare us the toil of looking for partial, individual answers to the question of meaning in our lives. And of course we must not be disappointed if our earthly history leaves us with but a very formal response to the global question of meaning—if in itself it fails to still our gnawing hunger for concrete, however particular and limited, meaning-fulfillment. The wish to have sugar in my coffee will not be satisfied by an explanation of God as the infinite Good and hence Vessel of all fulfillment.

The Search for Meaning

Before we speak of Jesus Christ as the meaning of life, we must make some clarifications. By "meaning," we of course do not intend particular individual connections among particular, concrete realities, in the manner of, for example, the recognizably "meaningful" connection between a bird's ability to fly and the construction of its wing—or even the insight that a given particular artistic experience, for example, has a meaning in itself, one that legitimates its existence apart from simple serviceability for something else. By "meaning," here, we intend the one, whole, universal, definitive meaning of all human existence. We presuppose that it is at least possible for there to be such meaning—that it is conceivable in nature and that it can be realized in the act of existence.

This presupposition is not a simple evidence. An agnostic or skeptic will say that human beings do indeed constantly undergo the experience of partial purposefulness and meaningfulness when they set themselves goals and realize them or strive for results which they consider to be positive or gratifying and pleasurable. But, our objectants will add, we cannot find and attain total, definitive meaning. Life ultimately melts away into emptiness, spills into the void. The search and demand for a definitive, all-encompassing meaning is senseless from the start.

The Christian is convinced of the contrary. He or she believes in the possibility of a comprehensive actualization of meaning, and believes that this actualization is the task of his or her own liberty, through the fulfillment of that human history which is the story of human freedom. At the same time the Christian believes this comprehensive meaning to be the gift of the one we call God—and that indeed it is only in positing an all-embracing fullness of meaning that it can dawn on anyone what is meant by the word "God."

Searching for a Meaning with Concrete Consequences

It would take us much too far afield to undertake to establish this basic conviction of Christians and to defend it as deserving of credence. Nevertheless there are two observations we must make concerning this total or global meaning.

First, it is immediately evident that the total, all-encompassing meaning of existence, which fulfills every requirement of a search for meaning, cannot be patched together of partial meanings. The search for a fulfillment of meaning would then yield nothing more than an endless series of partial meanings. Each would offer only the ever unfulfilled promise of a total fullness of meaning. The Christian seeks total meaning "outside the course of history," as everlasting life bestowed by God himself—even though this fullness of meaning is at the same time the eternal fruit of this history, in which it of course arises. Thus the Christian requires a meaning that must needs render all other possible answers unthinkable. The Christian answer is a "transcendent" one—and yet its validity is that of the only total answer for concrete living, for the life we have to live here and now. We may in no way blissfully consign the hope for eternity to the mystics and the dreamers, as if this earthly task of ours could suffer no changes under the influence of metaphysical dreams like those. For when, in earnest faith, we really and definitively "open up to God" and his eternal life as our only hope, then our relation to the realities and tasks of this world *will* undergo a change—and a liberating, unburdening change at that, a change that bestows on us the clear vision of the wide awake. But this, again, is something we cannot examine more closely here. Still we must hold firmly to the fact that our search for meaning, here and now, however surely its goal may be the God who overwhelms our practical experience, is not a question for idle speculation: it comports altogether real and tangible consequences.

Conversely, nevertheless, it is emphatically true that our global search for meaning does have God as its object—a God who is not a matter of our everyday experience, expecially in the form in which that experience is so narrowly shaped and molded by the spirit of modern empirical science. And yet, even in the presence of these limits and this narrowness, the problem of a metaphysical-existential (hence also in some way empirical) experience of God is far from deserving of a negative answer.

Meaning Become Mystery

Second, this God whom Christianity declares to be the fulfillment of the search for global meaning is the incomprehensible, impenetrable Mystery that can never be manipulated, and this he remains for all eternity. We cannot offer the basis for this proposition here. It shows why human perception is ultimately simply directed toward this mystery but "shatters"when it encounters it, if we may so speak, and only thus finds its fulfillment. But here we must simply presuppose the Christian conviction that God's incomprehensibility remains everlastingly mysterious. When all is said and done, the human being can aproach this incomprehensibility only in loving surrender and not by a perception that would drag the Perceived before some high tribunal charged with the perceiving of all reality.

But if God is the infinite Mystery that can never be comprehended, then the global search for meaning encounters a curious crisis. We cry for meaning, total meaning. And it is right that we should. In doing so, however, we are tempted almost involuntarily and unreflectively to understand this "meaning" as something "penetrable and penetrated," something illuminated and hence lighting up the darkness of our existence. We cry out for light, and unconsciously think of this Light, which is to illuminate all things and make them meaningful, after the fashion of our own lights, with which we go groping about in the dark. We think something is "perceived" or contacted by our knowledge only when the whole grid of all its little interconnections can clearly be seen, and the thing itself can now be inserted into the larger grid of our needs and inquisitiveness. But this is just what God in his incomprehensible mystery is *not* "all about." What our experience of perceiving the Incomprehensible constitutes is precisely *not* the pitiful leftovers of a perception that "sees through" things but the ultimate and primordial essence of perception itself.

When it is a matter of the total and definitive sense of human existence, and when this sense is to be the incomprehensible God, meaning becomes mystery, and we must surrender to it in mute, adoring love in order to approach it. This utterly different, unexpected signification makes no sense that we can see through, grasp, and bring into subjection. This sense is the mystery that closes *us* in its grasp. Its beatitude is bestowed on us only when we affirm and love this holy mystery for its own sake and not ours, when we surrender, and not when we surreptitiously seek to make God a means of our own self-affirmation.

The Search for Jesus

With the above as our point of departure, the question must now be broached whether and how Jesus Christ is the Christian response to the human search for meaning.

The proper and ultimate response to the search for meaning is of course God, in the way that we have just indicated. Now, inasmuch as we understand Jesus Christ to be the eternal Word of God, the proposition "Jesus Christ is the ultimate answer to the human being's search for meaning" is identical with the proposition that God is this answer—God and no one or anything else. But this is manifestly not what is meant by the proposition "Jesus Christ is the answer to the human being's search for meaning," for this would be nothing new, nothing particular or proper, nothing specifically Christian. Surely by "Jesus Christ" we mean the eternal Word of God. But we mean the eternal Word of God precisely *qua* incarnate, "become flesh," as John puts it—precisely as having entered into a real, substantial oneness with the whole human reality of Jesus of Nazareth.

Thus we are asking to what extent this Jesus of Nazareth, as a human being with a concrete human history, as someone died and risen, has what we shall call a constitutive significance for the sense of our life as total meaning. This will not simply coincide with the proposition that the eternal Word is the meaning of our life. Hence Jesus Christ, in his human reality and history, cannot be just as fully the global meaning of our existence as God is *qua* God.

Jesus' Humanity and the Total Meaning of the Human Being

This line of questioning is evidently of basic importance for Christian faith and life. On one hand, Jesus Christ in his humanity is not simply identical with God. He is one with God in the hypostatic union, but the hypostatic oneness in which we believe simultaneously expresses the distinction of the human and the divine reality. On the other hand, only God can be the human being's ultimate goal and meaning. It is surely an urgent question for Christians to know more precisely just what the humanity of Jesus betokens for the actual salvation—the total meaning—of the human being.

To be sure, this question is answered over and over again in Scripture, in Christian tradition and proclamation, in formulations that partly complement and partly simply repeat one another. Thus God is said to have assumed, in the incarnation of the eternal Word in Jesus of Nazareth, humanity in its entirety, and thus by taking on our nature to have entered into solidarity with all humanity. Or: the eternal Word has redeemed us in the passion and obedient death of his human history, as it is through these that he has made satisfaction to God's everlasting justice and thereby become the ground of God's salvific will—the basis for God's addressing to us, in spite of humanity's sinfulness, his forgiving grace that is himself. Or again: Jesus of Nazareth is in some way the historical event that is not only supported and maintained by the eternal, transhistorical God, like any other history, but the event in whom God himself deals with the world on the stage of history, suffering its tragedy with it to the end. Or finally: through the obedience of his passion, as the absolutely innocent and lovingly pure one, Jesus Christ has opened for us the way to the Father, for he has entered into absolute and complete solidarity with us.

These expressions and conceptions of the salvific meaning of Jesus Christ—of his constitutive meaning and function for the total sense of our existence—are but a few of the many such formulations that may be found.*

Now, the soteriological declarations of Christian tradition may be divided into those which we can range more or less under a "pure Chalcedonianism," and those which would be more likely to go under "neo-Chalcedonianism." These are merely abstruse, technical theological formulations for the following. Many theologians understand the oneness of divinity and humanity as the ground of salvation so emphatically *as* oneness that, while maintaining the Chalcedonian doctrine of the nonconfusion, or noncommingling, of divinity and humanity in Jesus, they nevertheless proceed to regard Jesus' history and lot as the history and lot of God *as God*. Thus they interpret the Chalcedonian dogma in the manner of Cyril of Alexandria: God has suffered; the eternal Word of God has himself undergone our condition and our death and thereby our condition and our death are saved and redeemed; the Word of the Father has personally taken on our condition, with its mortgage of sin and death, and thereby redeemed it.

This neo-Chalcedonian salvation theory has its representatives in theology today as well, although to be sure they generally do not make explicit appeal to neo-Chalcedonianism itself. Its expressions and propositions belong per se to Catholic Christianity's deposit of faith, for they contain, as far as they go, the *communicatio*

---

*Here we are prescinding from the frequent and legitimate distinction of such formulations into propositions that apply more ontic concepts and schemata, and those that apply more "moral" ones—into expressions, then, of an ontological unity, a unity of being, of the Word with the creature, which in themselves are now not conceived simply as preliminaries to salvation but as constitutive of salvation—or into other expressions, of sacrifice, blood, obedience, and so on, which alone are seen to constitute the salvation event in the proper sense.

idiomatum—the doctrine that everything that can be said of Jesus as a human being is also predicable of Jesus-Christ-who-is-God (not "insofar as he is God"!). But a fine distinction, difficult to discern and yet of far-reaching consequence, arises in this neo-Chalcedonianism as we have just described it, the moment these expressions are read in the sense of a pure Chalcedonianism, which insists on the nonconfusion of the two natures.

The neo-Chalcedonian presentation would, while respecting the mystery, understand redemption as a matter of God's having suffered, God's having died, and thereby having redeemed us. While not forgetting that we are dealing with a mystery here, the neo-Chalcedonian understands the expression "Jesus was obedient unto death" of the divinity itself, as well as of the humanity. A representative of pure Chalcedonianism, however, while continuing to maintain the hypostatic union of divinity and humanity in Jesus, will insist here that, in this union of divinity and humanity, the nonconfusion must also be safeguarded. Death and finitude belong only to the creaturely reality of Jesus. They remain "this side" of the infinite distance separating God and creature; they remain on the creaturely side of the one "God-man." The eternal Word, in his *divinity*, can undergo no such historicity nor any "obedience unto death."

Pure Chalcedonianism is ever wary of the other soteriology, fearing it will make the surreptitious transition from a *communicatio idiomatum*, a communication or exchange of concrete attributes (in the two natures) precisely to an *identity* of concrete attributes (of both natures). We would then have the eternal, impassible God, who transcends all history—in a spirit of gnosticism or Schellingism or what you will—suffering in himself, suffering as God. We would be positing the redemption of our condition as occurring in virtue of a transposition of that condition to the interiority of God himself. Pure Chalcedonianism, while maintaining the hypostatic union, and thereby the validity of the *communicatio idiomatum* (but understood in a Chalcedonian way), will emphasize that finitude and death are the prime constituents of the condition from which we are to be redeemed—that we are redeemed from them by their being Jesus' condition as well—and that in him they can indeed be rightly predicated of the Word too, because of the hypostatic union, but not in such a way as to posit this subject and predicate, the eternity of the divinity and the passion of the humanity, in an identity. The dogma of the hypostatic union expresses a unity, a oneness, that is unique, not occurring elsewhere, unknown to us in any other instance, and including within itself the distinction and nonconfusion that was proclaimed as dogma at Chalcedon.

From "Christ for Us" to "Christ in Himself"

But then the theologians of pure Chalcedonianism are left with the question as to how this oneness of God and the human being may be the bearer of a function and meaning for redemption. The question remains how we are redeemed, if God has burdened the human reality of Jesus with our existential condition of guilt and death. Jesus' lot is God's lot in a true sense. But this lot, this history and condition, leaves God's own life, with its transhistoricity, impassibility, and innocent beatitude, untouched. God's reality and Jesus' creatureliness remain "unconfused," uncommingled. The pure Chalcedonian will always hold that it is God's impassible, holy blessedness that has "formally" redeemed us—not something earthly and finite that has been speculatively introduced into the interiority of God *qua* God. He or she will say that Jesus' death, however it is ultimately to be explained, can alone be the reason why, and rationale how, God gives us his own blessedness as our own. It cannot in itself be ("formally," then) this redemption.

Our rather lengthy excursus here on neo-Chalcedonian soteriology is not intended as a denial that the doctrine of the hypostatic union is the basis of the soteriological meaning of Jesus' history and a necessary element in salvation itself. But the question remains whether an understanding of christological dogma, including the hypostatic union, would not be better served by an approach from just the opposite pole from that with which traditional theology begins: whether it would not be better to begin not with Jesus' divinity, not with the hypostatic union, and thence proceed to the reality of salvation, but to begin with the soteriological significance for us of Jesus and his history, and there begin our search for an understanding of the meaning of the hypostatic union.

The path we are proposing, then, leads from "Christ for us" to

"Christ in himself." Let us put it very simply. The hypostatic union will be understood here as the presupposition, perhaps not a very readily clarified one, for what we experience in Jesus: that he is the last, irrevocable word of God's forgiveness and self-bestowal upon us. The Christian dogma of Jesus as both God and human being will be understood as a formulation of Jesus' unique, irreplaceable meaning for salvation for us, and the hypostatic union is thereby the presupposition inseparably contained in this proposition about Jesus' meaning for salvation.

Jesus Christ, the Meaning and Salvation of Human Existence

In order to present Jesus' unsurpassable and definitive salvation-meaning in a way we can grasp, let us start out quite "from below." Here is a human being who lives in an attitude of matchless nearness to God—someone who lives in pure obedience to God and at the same time in unconditional solidarity with human beings, regardless of how the latter may behave toward him. This two-way solidarity, with God and with human beings, is maintained by Jesus unconditionally, to the limit. The historical outcome of this for Jesus is his death—in which he definitively and totally surrenders to God and God's incomprehensible disposition, while steadfastly maintaining his unconditional love for human beings as well. In this plunge into the helplessness of death, however, he becomes the definitively Affirmed and Accepted One, *and* this is how he is experienced by us: as the Risen One. (This is the Christian faith, going back to the experience of Jesus' disciples and of the Church, and we cannot undertake an express legitimation of it here.)

Thus the fate and person of Jesus have a special, proper meaning, above and beyond their ordinary human character. This Jesus proclaims that, with himself, the definitive, irrevocable address of God's forgiving and self-bestowing love is present—that the Kingdom of God has irrevocably come, that the victory of God's forgiving love in the history of human kind is complete and irreversible insofar as God himself is concerned. And in God's definitive acceptance of Jesus through his resurrection, Jesus' claim to be the vehicle of God's definitive self-communication to the world, despite its sin and finitude and mortality, is legitimated and sealed.

But then, in his self-interpretation, in his death, and in his resurrection, Jesus is the matchless, definitive word of God's testimony to himself in the world. If we understand this to the hilt, we have the traditional doctrine of the substantial, hypostatic union of the Word with the human reality of Jesus. If we accept Jesus as God's irreversible, definitive self-bestowal on us, thereby we shall be confessing him as the consubstantial Son of God.

How is this to be explained? Any creaturely, finite reality emerges from a broader field of possibilities. Alongside this reality there are other, noncontradictory possibilities which could be, or could have been, realized as well, or instead. In this one actualized possibility alone, God, its free creator, is never definitively committed. Everything finite and historical, considered as such and in itself, is subject to recall, is ever the object of a divine liberty that never posits itself absolutely, as indeed it is unable to, through this finite thing as such alone. Therefore any revelation in which God objectifies and manifests his will through a finite word or historical event remains, *a parte post*, open, subject to revision, and provisional.

Nothing simply finite is capable, as such and in itself alone, of signifying and transmitting to us an unsurpassable communication of God. It is ever provisional among the infinitude of God's opportunities and the sovereignty of his freedom. Thus if God communicates his self-affirmation to us as an irrevocable and definitive self-affirmation, then the creaturely reality through which he does so cannot simply stand at the same distance from him as other creaturely realities. The creaturely reality must in this instance be God's own reality, in such unique wise that God would be effectively cancelling *himself*, were he ever to surpass it in virtue of its creaturely finitude.

Only a finite reality that is assumed by God as his own reality can make God's commitment in the world irrevocable. The revelatory word of God to us, when it is to be unsurpassable, must be God's own reality—else it will remain trapped in the conditionality and surpassability peculiar to things finite. A mere prophet can surely speak in God's name. But the finite message he or she communicates by deed and word can only proclaim something that is open *a parte post* and surpassable. To put it in biblical terms: Only

the Son who *is* God's word, and who announces it not in mere finitude alone, can be the definitive, ultimate, no longer surpassable
prophet. But Jesus claims to be God's definitive, unconditional, irreversible self-commitment, and this self-interpretation and claim
of his are endorsed and confirmed by God through the definitiveness of his existence, in death and resurrection. Accordingly, his human reality, with its historicity and finitude intact, must be not
merely *posited* by the God of the other world, but must be that
God's own reality—however difficult we may find it to discern
whence it comes that a divine reality that is God in identity can be
distinguished from a reality of God that is God by acceptance—that is, in oneness, but without being one and the same.

If these considerations are correct in their basic intent, despite
any imperfections they may comport in their formulation, then
we can say: Jesus is the consubstantial Son of God; his human reality, without prejudice to its genuine, free, human subjectivity, is
that of the eternal Word of God—for Jesus is the irrevocable, unsurpassable, and definitive self-commitment of God to us; and this
he can only be as God's consubstantial Son.

Faith in Jesus Christ
Now it is clear how altogether possible it is to have a Christology
that begins with the experience of Jesus, that begins "from below,"
that experiences him as our salvation—that is, that encounters
him as the historical experience of God's self-bestowal. From here
we can proceed quite readily to the metaphysical propositions of
classic Christology. The proposition that Jesus is God's definitive
self-commitment to us, and the proposition that Jesus is the incarnate Word of God, are interchangeable, provided only the first
proposition be taken in radical earnest, and the second be understood in a Chalcedonian, and not monophysitical, sense as being a
proposition about the true *oneness* or *unity* of the Word and the
human reality of Jesus, and not as a proposition of simple identity.

There is an ascending, or "low," Christology—a Christology
that begins with the human Jesus—that complements the classic
descending, or "high," Christology of God become a human being. The former clarifies how and why a seemingly innocuous relationship of unconditional trust in Jesus can be charged with the

whole of classic Christology. It shows that such a relationship is altogether available to the ordinary Christian who is not a professional theologian, and that indeed it can be expected of him or her. To be sure, it is desirable that such a Christian have a certain acquaintance with the formulations of classic Christology, and if he or she is educated this is to be expected. But if he or she finds this a difficulty and experiences, shall we say, a "metaphysical overload," he or she need not consider himself or herself a poor Christian, or one of doubtful orthodoxy.

If a Christian can trustingly and confidently say; "In Jesus of Nazareth, in his life, his teaching, his catastrophic death, his victory (which we call his resurrection), God has given me himself—his forgiveness, his own life, above and beyond all finite fulfillment—if a Christian believes that this self-bestowal of God's is unconditional, irreversible, and definitive for his own part, and that it can never be superseded or surpassed in some new age to come—for indeed, as God's last word it *can* no longer be superseded—if a Christian is engaged and committed to this in a free outpouring of faith, and allows this matchless hope more validity than all doubts, skepticism, and reservations—then he or she is an orthodox Christian. This Christian experiences classic Christology existentially. This Christian finds and accepts Jesus, actually understood, and rightly understood, as his or her salvation.

WHO ARE
YOUR BROTHER
AND SISTER?

Preface

This little essay reproduces essentially the text of an address I delivered on November 10, 1980, to the Catholic university community and the Catholic academicians of Graz, on the campus of the university in that city. I had been asked to speak on *Brüderlichkeit*, "brotherhood," which was the theme of the Diocesan Day of Recollection of the Diocese of Graz-Seckau.

The length of an hour to which I had to limit my presentation posed a problem. What could be said on a subject of such immeasurable importance and breadth in so short a time?

And so the content of this address, which I have revised for publication, may strike the reader as consisting of rather arbitrarily selected, random thoughts on the subject of who one's brothers and sisters are. And I must confess that this is indeed the case. But I hope that these thoughts will be welcomed in the spirit in which they are offered—as a gift from a brother. After all, a communion of brothers and sisters in the Church is something precious, and something to be nurtured, by one another and for one another.

Introduction

As the title "Who Are Your Brother and Sister?" will suggest, we propose in the following pages to treat Christian *fraternitas*—the Christian communion of brothers and sisters—in its essence as well as in its contemporary possibilities and difficulties. But this subject is so boundless, so general that there is a great danger we shall be speaking, in the selections we shall inevitably have to make, just precisely of what the reader does not expect. It may be, then, that this book will disappoint and frustrate that reader, and that he or she will lay it aside. But this is a danger we shall have to live with.

First we shall set forth certain general *theological considerations* (chapter 1). Then we shall observe that, for a Christian communion of brothers and sisters, we have an altogether *new situation* today (chapter 2). Finally we shall draw, from these two series of considerations, certain *conclusions* for our actual Christian life (chapter 3).

1 · Preliminary Considerations

Love for God and Human Beings
Let us open our discussion of the love of neighbor with some observations on the basic relationship between love for God and love for human beings.

In the popular Christian conception, as expressed in the average sermon or religion lesson (not that there will not sometimes be exceptions), this relationship is seen too superficially. We hear a genuine, salvific relationship to God propounded in summary terms as "a love of God above all things." Then we are informed that this relationship requires the observance of God's commandments, without which God cannot be loved aright. And one of these commandments is the commandment of love of neighbor.

If this is the way in which we understand the connection between love of God and love of neighbor, the latter can seem both relatively self-evident and very difficult. Thus it can be pictured as a kind of "test case" of one's love for God in practical life. But this is a very superficial way of understanding the relationship between love of God and love of neighbor.

Love of God as the Only Thing and Everything
In the first place, the essence of the love of God is already almost inevitably misunderstood when that love is thought of as the observance of an individual, particular commandment—one commandment among others. No, just as God is not rightly understood when he is thought of simply as a particular reality, a partial reality in the sum total of all realities, so also the love of God may

69

not be degraded to the status of a particular achievement among a plurality of things to be achieved in human existence. The love of God is the totality of the free fulfillment of human existence. It is not, in the last analysis, the content of an individual commandment, but is at once the basis and the goal of all individual commandments. And it is what it must be only when God is loved for his own sake—when love for him is produced and experienced not with a view to human self-assertion and interior self-fulfillment, in the accomplishment of certain individual exploits which people require of themselves, but when human beings, ultimately without self-seeking, go out of themselves, forget themselves because of God, and really lose themselves in the ineffable mystery to which they willingly surrender.

The human being attains his or her fulfillment in one single, total act of his or her existence: in the love of God for his own sake. But this fulfillment is, precisely, only reached when not it but God is sought. Inasmuch as such love is the whole of the fulfillment of human existence, there is nothing more self-evident than it, since only a whole, and not a part, is self-explanatory—only a whole can be understood in itself. At the same time, however, inasmuch as this love is surrender to God, a surrender to the never-to-be-comprehended, a surrender to that which remains mystery for all eternity—this self-evident love is at the same time incomprehensible in itself. That is, it is not resolvable into elements that are better understood in separation. When love of God is lauded from the pulpit as the condition of salvation, it is not a particular achievement on the part of human beings that is meant, but the one total self-fulfillment of the human being, at once self-evident and incomprehensible, in which the human being dispossesses himself or herself in self-abandonment to God.

When we consider all this—and yet at the same time experience this curved-in-on-itself subjectivity of ours that ever seeks itself as its end and goal—then such a love of God for his own sake, this eruption, this breaking out of the locked-up narrowness of our own existence, necessarily appears to us as a miracle, which ultimately only God himself can bestow upon us. When we hope for the salvation of all humankind, what we are hoping for is this unspeakable wonder of the love of God for us, which itself bestows upon us the very thing that is the sole salvific deed of our lives. This love is to be hoped for against and despite all manifestations of a hugely sinful (or most sublime) selfishness on the part of the human being.

It is this real love for God that must be kept in view, as we now proceed to ask ourselves about the relationship between love for God and love for neighbor. It is this true, genuine love of God that we shall be speaking of, and not some individual, particular moral exploit.

The Reciprocal Relationship Between Love of God and Love of Neighbor

The relationship of the love of God to a love of neighbor is not merely in virtue of the fact that a love of neighbor is commanded by it and functions somehow as a practical test case for it. The relationship is much more intimate than that. Love of God and love of neighbor stand in a relationship of mutual conditioning. Love of neighbor is not only a love that is demanded by the love of God, an achievement flowing from it; it is also in a certain sense its antecedent condition.

This relationship of mutual conditioning, of mutual inclusion, must not of course be understood in the sense of a secular humanism, as if love for God were only an old-fashioned, mythological expression for love of neighbor—so that, when all is said and done, one could simply skip over it today if one could still maintain an inexorable, unselfish love for human beings without it. No, God is more than a human being—infinitely more. He is the loving God to whom the human being reaches out in adoration across all human reality. And yet a mutual relationship does obtain between love of God and love of neighbor, in their real mutual conditioning. There is no love for God that is not, in itself, already a love for neighbor; and love for God only comes to its own identity through its fulfillment in a love for neighbor. Only one who loves his or her neighbor can know who God actually is. And only one who ultimately loves God (whether he or she is reflexively aware of this or not is another matter) can manage unconditionally to abandon himself or herself to another person, and not make that person the means of his or her own self-assertion.

At the same time, the fact that love for God is already actually present, therefore, in unconditional love for one's neighbor does not imply any diminishment or falsification of a genuine love for the neighbor. God is not in competition with human beings. God is the one who renders human beings intelligible, gives them their ultimate, radical value and meaning, by being utterly interior to them, and yet infinitely surpassing them, all at the same time. "Existence into God" is human beings' inmost interiority. In being "loved forth into God," so to speak, human beings are loved in their ultimate meaning and essence. And in genuinely opening themselves to their neighbor, they receive the possibility of going forth from themselves, coming out of themselves and loving God.

This mutual relationship of the love of God and the love of neighbor ought really to be plumbed in much more precision and depth if one hopes to gain any understanding of what a Christian communion of brothers and sisters must mean. Since, after all, this Christian *fraternitas* is really only another term for love of neighbor, and since love of neighbor, in turn, embraces the mystery of a love for God which is the totality of the true fulfillment of one's existence—then this incomprehensibility, which is also self-evident, must be kept in account as we continue to consider, in the pages which follow, this very *fraternitas*—this Christian communion of brothers and sisters.

The Unity of Disposition and Act
For Catholic philosophical anthropology, there is both a unity and a distinction between disposition and its act. By act, we understand a concrete, indicable, verifiable accomplishment, capable of being delimited, defined, and organized. Disposition, ultimately and really, denotes a human being's single, total relationship to God and neighbor. Disposition and act, or deed, may neither be separated nor identified. A final disposition is really only itself when it concretizes itself in an act—without, however, thereby becoming absolutely graspable, verifiable, in itself. Rather, disposition, when it concretizes itself in act, brings itself both to the self-manifestation that it requires and to a certain hiddenness, inasmuch as, in its necessary objectivization-in-act, it nevertheless

cannot be adequately grasped and fixed for the reflection of the agent of the deed and that of other observers.

In view of this relationship of disposition and act in unity and distinction, an ethics of disposition and an ethics of accomplishment cannot be considered as two ultimately identical quantities, such that one could simply choose between them. Hence also, as far as love of neighbor, a Christian communion of brothers and sisters, is concerned, no choice may be permitted between an ethics of disposition and an ethics of accomplishment either. Disposition may not dispense with deed, but neither is disposition acquitted or discharged through exploit and accomplishment.

The Historical Guise of Love of Neighbor

Love of neighbor exhibits a true historicity, a genuine historical actualization. Concrete love of neighbor, necessarily and constantly, takes on ever new forms in history, one after another, in accordance with the diversity of human beings and their varying historical situations. But history and historical development are not simply the development, the unfolding, of what is known to have gone before. History is always providing surprises. The same will be true, then, for the history of Christian love of neighbor. It too will constantly be confronted with new situations—with which it has never had to reckon until now, situations that have not always been represented in traditional, customary Christian religious discourse as this discourse moves down from generation to generation. There is a genuine historicity of Christian love of neighbor. This is why the Church too is constantly encountering new surprises in this area—colliding with demands and tasks for the love of neighbor alive within it with which it has never had to reckon before, tasks which it has simply never preached from the pulpit in the "good old days"—tasks whose moment for Christianity has come but slowly to Christian consciousness.

Basically, this state of affairs goes without saying, given the historicity of humanity and the genuine historicity of the Church and its preaching of the gospel. It is not as if one had but to open the gospel to be able to read, in all clarity and simplicity, what love of neighbor and the disposition for a communion of brothers and sisters has as its task today. But there is a traditionalism that thinks, in varying degrees of explicitness, that the only demands which love of neighbor can make are those that have always been expressly preached. The truth of the matter, however, is that tasks and demands of love of neighbor are making themselves known today that no pastoral letter of a hundred years ago ever mentioned, and yet that are as pressing today as the ancient injunctions against stealing one's neighbor's property. Demands of Christian nonviolence, environmental protection, responsible family planning, health care, political responsibility, and so forth, can be of at least as much moment as the particular injunctions of Christian love of neighbor that have been reflected upon and preached in the past as the content of the commandment to love one's neighbor.

2 · Addressing a New Situation

A New Situation for Christian Communion

The first proposition, and a simple one, among our actual considerations on Christian love of neighbor, or a Christian communion of brothers and sisters, could be formulated as follows: The Christian communion of brothers and sisters today has entered a new phase. The very substitution of the word *fraternitas* for "love of neighbor" is already a little indication of this.

When we say that a Christian communion of brothers and sisters has entered today into a new historical situation, we do not mean, to be sure, that one can time it with a stopwatch and see just when "today" began. A new historical phase may develop slowly. It may announce its inception beforehand in many ways and not simply suddenly appear (and yet it will basically be quite clearly given) in such a way as to be perceived reflexively by the common consciousness of the Church as something altogether new on its horizon. Rather, the past is not simply snuffed out: it continues to be present in its elements as necessarily or factually continuing to survive, and thereby it masks, for the myopia of human awareness, the novelty of the actual situation.

But there are, by all means, greater and lesser changes in the situation of the Church—changes not only in the Church's outward, profane situation, but changes which form inner moments of historical transformation in the Church as well (without prejudice to the Church's abiding essential identity). The transition of the Church from a Jewish-Christian era to one of a gentile Christianity, the transformation of the Church from a patristic culture to a western medieval Christianity—but also, for example, the laborious change in the Church that was set afoot at the Enlightenment—are situations of this sort and are of a most penetrating nature. What we may characterize as democracy, in a rationally technological age, an age of the steadily intensifying oneness of world civilization, the meaning of the emancipation of women, and much more, all belong on the list. These changes of situation develop slowly and in certain circumstances collide with heavy resistence, even in the Church, especially in a very traditional Christianity in the Church. And even when they succeed in establishing themselves, they are still fused with the remnants of tasks left uncompleted.

This new situation in the Church, which we need not describe in fuller detail here, has great importance for a Christian communion of brothers and sisters. The change in situation arising for such *fraternitas* with the overall new current situation may perhaps be characterized in a twofold way: It is the situation of a global, unified, "standardized" humanity, and it is the situation of a new kind of interiority for human beings.

A Humanity Gradually Becoming One

The situation in which we live today is that of a humanity that is gradually unifying—ever more tightly coalescing. Of course, this is not to say that this gradually unifying historical world of human beings, with all the global interdependence of its joint cultural realities—its ways of thinking and acting, its secular scientific knowledge and technological know-how—is by any means a world of harmony and peace. On the contrary, we now live in a world in which, despite the fact that the individual histories of its peoples and cultures are no longer separated by empty geographical spaces, conflictual situations are actually becoming much more dangerous and threatening than they were in ancient times.

But there is a unity, a oneness, of humanity that has only come to be, slowly but surely, in our modern times. The Mongol scourge, or the siege of Vienna by the Turks three hundred years ago, were certainly mighty events of the deepest significance for our Western history. But they were of no real immediate moment for the history of Southeast Asia. Today, a historical event occurring at any point on the surface of the earth has its weight and meaning for the weal and woe of every other particular historical space. There is a centripetal force at work in humanity today, driving individual cultural and historical spaces together—in varying degrees, to be sure—into a single, common existential space for all human beings.

We might point to the story of the tower of Babel in Genesis as an illustration that, for the Old Testament's theology of history, the division of peoples was a providential method of the divine governance of history, antecedent to human beings' decision, for forestalling rebellion against God as a generalized human phenomenon. And from this point of departure we could well ask ourselves the theological meaning of a humanity heretofore scattered and divided, but now reaching a unity of the interdependence of all upon all again, so that, for example, only today has an organized atheism come to be the official state religion of broad sectors of humanity. We might ask what the various elements are that have brought us to this unification of humanity. We might show how it has been only with this unification of humanity that a general and generally accepted (at least in notion and challenge) humanism has prevailed, one that has facilitated a promulgation of "human rights" that only today, after all, have become a real program for the Church.

Christian Communion in a New World Church

In this new situation for humanity we also have a new situation for the Church and its communion of brothers and sisters. The Church can and must now genuinely become a world Church in the modern sense of the term, and hence live its communion in an altogether new, heretofore nonexistent manner.

In the wake of European colonialism, beginning in the sixteenth century, the Church in our times has taken upon itself the task of a world mission. But up to the present the Christianity it has sought to bring the world has been transmitted, innocently and inevitably, pretty much as a European export. We have to admit that our brothers and sisters in lands outside the West have been treated, unintentionally, as underaged children in a family. We have formed them in a Latin theology, given them a Latin liturgy, built them neo-Gothic churches in Japan, had them singing European hymns, and given them European bishops, or native bishops chosen for them in Rome to European specifications.

This may all have been well intentioned, and entirely unavoidable (although of course we Europeans, sinful Christians that we are, must at the same time admit to a measure of European arrogance and presumptuousness in these matters). But today, in the age of a uniform humanity, a humanity that seeks to accord all its members equal rights and majority of age, the Church may no longer permit itself to remain a European Church exporting Western Christianity to the whole world. Now it must really become a world Church. And the performance of this task is a new form, present today in virtue of our new situation, of the Christian communion which ought to prevail among the churches and human beings that together make up the one Church. Not that the unity of the Church, its origin the world over from Jewish and Western beginnings, and its center in Rome, need be denied or glossed over. But communion as a Christian challenge today has become concretized in the task of realizing in our own times a genuine world Church.

To be sure, the accomplishment of this task has already begun, in the Second Vatican Council and everything that led to and prepared for that Council. For the first time in history, a world episcopate gathered in council. For the first time, representatives of nearly every people and culture on earth have actively cooperated in Church decisions. Theology today is no longer the neoscholasticism of the nineteenth and first half of the twentieth centuries. The surrender of Latin as the official language of the Church for the whole world has laid the groundwork for pluralism in the liturgy, which we must have if a single world Church is to be made up of brothers and sisters and of local and regional churches really having equal rights. But there is still a great deal to be done in the area of equal rights for all of our brothers and sisters in one Church, and we still have a long way to go before we shall have dismantled a Western supremacy throughout the Church.

Indeed there is the danger, and there are already symptoms, of a regression in this development of the Church toward a genuine world Church in our times. The long-awaited new Code of Canon Law threatens to be a Roman canon law for the entire world. The initiatives under way in the great continental churches (in Latin America, Asia, Africa), whereby these churches attempt to identify and carry out new, special tasks of their own with a view to a genuine inculturation of Christianity, or the exercise of a new sociopolitical responsibility, instead of being encouraged in Rome, seem to have had cold water thrown on them.

A communion of brothers and sisters that credibly and trustworthily meets the needs of the human beings and local and regional churches that make up one Church—a communion that does not keep them under anxious surveillance, a communion that encourages them to actualize concrete expressions of what it means to be Christian, expressions which will perhaps at first alienate us Westerners and be all but unintelligible to us—still has a good many assignments to confront before a truly adequate brotherly and sisterly spirit in the Church can become objective reality.

Strange as it may sound, the outcome of the world's growing uniformity for the Church is more pluralism in the Church. Only pluralism can really actualize equal brotherly and sisterly rights among all Christians and all individual churches. The uniformity of the European Church, which may once upon a time have been impossible to avoid, must now yield to the genuine oneness of a world Church. But this oneness, this unity, is only capable of being realized if a brotherly and sisterly attitude, devoid of any paternalistic arrogance, is willing to accord an equality of rights to all members of the Church.

A World of Intercommunication

A further particularity of Christian communion in today's situation resides, it seems to me, in today's increased opportunities for intercommunication among persons. What I mean by this is not easy to explain, and perhaps a brief word of clarification is in order.

When we reflect on the possibilities people of earlier times had for exchanging the content of their consciousnesses, in awareness and freedom, we cannot deny that their opportunities were most restricted in comparison with ours today. Generally people could neither read nor write. There were no newspapers nor any other real communications media. Further, the scope of existing knowledge, in comparison with what is objectively known today in all the sciences, and subjectively assimilable, was unbelievably small, great and meaningful as the ancient knowledge of the sages of the past may have been. Means of research into people's subjectivity have greatly increased in reach and sophistication. Access to the consciousness of the "other" is much more open than it ever was before. Today's human being has become more "communicable," because he or she has become more expressive.

To be sure, in this area as in others, it is possible to abuse new opportunities that arise instead of using them honorably and properly. All these potentialities for intercommunication today have been promptly abused and placed in the service of mass manipulation—the cunning control of the general consciousness—by agencies that acknowledge no responsibility for their actions, for purposes of anonymous brainwashing, even in ostensibly democratic societies.

As for the *good* use of all these opportunities, Christians hobble along behind what others make of them. The Church's "propaganda apparatus," if we may so term it, still seems very old-fashioned. What it all comes down to is the question of the feasibility of putting these new means of broader and more intensive intercommunication to work in the service of a deeper and more vital communion of brothers and sisters. Of course, we already see beginnings. Today a Christian who is in some measure involved in the life of the Church knows more—and knows it more graphically and vividly—about his or her brothers and sisters in foreign lands, and about their Christian life with its challenges and its difficulties, through classes and lectures, through what he or she hears on the radio or watches on television, by journeys to foreign lands, than was possible for the average Christian of earlier times. And since we know more about these far-off brothers and sisters, we can help them more energetically, by prayer, by financial assistance, and by real, clearly expressed participation in their Christian and ecclesial life. These new opportunities for intraChurch communion impose on us a greater responsibility to bring today's new potentialities to realization, to the enhancement of our communion of brothers and sisters, as energetically as possible. For as real possibilities, these opportunities become tasks to accomplish.

Brotherly and Sisterly Encounter

But it seems to me that, besides the new opportunities for brotherly and sisterly intercommunication that we have already mentioned, there are other, altogether different opporunities as well, which transform themselves into requirements of two-way nearness, and call for fulfillment on our part. Surely we have seen some very intense forms of human nearness and intercommunication in mutual love in earlier times. But in comparison with what is possible today, the opportunities of times gone by were in many respects very restricted indeed. Living and suffering side by side with others was in many respects much more a matter of quiet discretion than it is today. Indeed, religion and Christian spirituality were often developed more as a way of enduring one's loneliness in the company of God alone as much as might be. Today, then, there arises the possibility of making recently developed potentialities for social intercommunication effective for a brotherly and sisterly exchange of personal spirituality as well—for discovering the will of God in our own individual lives, and for sharing genuine Christian courage and consolation with one another through God's Spirit. Common prayer in charismatic groups is certainly one possible way of fostering this Christian communion—a way which, while it has always been basically possible, has demonstrated new potential, hence new demands, in the context of today's new opportunities for intercommunication.

Of course, there is one last, lonely responsibility and deed to be done, in a freedom which ultimately cannot be shared or transferred, and it is one of the essentials of Christian spirituality. When all is said and done, it is each of us individually—all communion and love of neighbor aside for the moment (though concretely it will have been precisely in virtue of this communion and love of neighbor)—who must become this particular person, of whom there is only one, and who only as this unique individual can manage an ultimate contribution to the actualization of the communion of saints. For the communion of saints is not built up by scooping together samples of the human species. But this is not to deny that we have a situation today in which a sublime communion of brothers and sisters, in a concretely actualized community of the Spirit and of love, is a new possibility and challenge. Perhaps there are opportunities here for the Church and its spirituality that are still beyond our imaginings today. Not that one need be a Marxist socialist, but if there are tasks of socialization of the human being incumbent upon us in secular society that are still far from realization, then perhaps we have something left to do along these lines in the Church as well. There may be forms of higher socialization possible which for all practical purposes still go unrecognized in our reflexive consciousness, and which would have the potential to raise those forms of ecclesial intercommunication of which we are conscious, and from which we so often suffer, to new heights. Finally, it is entirely conceivable that we may have neglected and allowed to atrophy forms of intercommunication and ecclesial community life (for example, in the liturgy and received Church usage) with which we are familiar from our tradition, but whose potentialities for a genuine brotherly and sisterly intercommunication we have underestimated.

There has prevailed, in the mentality and spirituality of secular society and the Church, even to our own day, a certain subjectivity (which has somehow been considered an absolute), resting upon itself, and closed in upon itself, as if it went without saying that this is the way it should be, which has experienced the physical proximity of human beings in the Church rather as a vague, somewhat unpleasant concession to be made, instead of as an authentic actualization of the spiritual life. Even if we in the Church do not wish to become precisely "spiritual socialists," still we should not say that this individualistic mentality of the nineteenth century, which was unquestionably accepted in broad sectors of the Church, holds the promise of everlasting validity and durability. An interior, primordial spirituality does not necessarily involve a self-sufficient subjectivity. Those who still cope with themselves and their spiritual task today, in spite of the Church's new style for these modern times, in as complete an isolation as possible, may be under no obligation to change themselves, if you will, but at least they should make room for others to practice a different, more brotherly and sisterly lifestyle, even in matters spiritual.

3 · Consequences

Dangers of True Communion

Christian love of neighbor, a Christian communion of brothers and sisters, receives an altogether new status and an altogether new value when it is lived as a concrete manner of actualizing love for God instead of being understood only as a secondary requirement and obligation imposed on us as a commandment by God. In our average Christian life, however, it looks as if what we must attend to is basically only our own salvation, through prayer, reception of the sacraments, participation in the eucharist, and the avoidance or expiation of sin—and in the process, of course, and for the same purpose, through avoiding massive offenses against the obligation we have regarding our neighbor. But would not the Christian life look entirely different if we spontaneously and unquestioningly heard "Save your soul" as "Save your neighbor"?

When we look at the average Christian life, it would seem that the notion prevailing in the normal Christian's moral consciousness is that we have "loved our neighbor" when we have done nothing evil to him or her, and have met the objective claims he or she may justly have against us. The truth, however, is that what we are commanded by the "commandment" to love our neighbor, in its oneness with the commandment to love God, is the demolition of our own selfishness—the overthrow of the notion that love of neighbor is basically really only the rational settlement of mutual claims, that it demands only giving and taking to the mutual satisfaction of all parties. In reality, Christian love of neighbor attains its true essence only where no more accounts are kept—where

83

a readiness prevails to love without requital—where, in the love of neighbor as well, the folly of the cross is accepted and welcomed.

When one really understands the unity of the love of God and neighbor, the latter shifts from its position as a particular demand for a delimited, verifiable achievement to a position of total fulfillment of one's life, in which we are challenged in our totality, wholly challenged, challenged beyond our capacity—but challenged in the only way in which we may gain the highest freedom: freedom from ourselves. Thus if we understand love of God and a brotherly/sisterly communion as two expressions denoting basically the same thing—and if we say "communion of brothers and sisters" rather than "love of neighbor" because this expression is less likely than the other to be misunderstood as a demand for a factual, neutral accomplishment that dispenses the heart from its last obligation—then we may safely say that with a communion of brothers and sisters, in its necessary oneness with the love of God, we have expressed the single totality of the task of the whole human being and of Christianity.

But now our expression "communion of brothers and sisters" will have to defend itself against a certain maudlin, sentimental misinterpretation. For are we not now challenged in a way calculated to throw the normal Christian consciousness into a state of considerable commotion? In consternation, must we not wonder: Have I ever, ever once, loved in such a manner that no echo, no reward, no recognition, no self-attestation or endorsement answered this love? Have I even once in my life loved with the terrible feeling that I was nothing but stupid, simply made a fool of and used?

These experiences, these tests of unselfish love, to be sure, leave something to be desired with respect to a cheery, blissful experience. But wherever a human being, in his or her love, is unable mutely and unquestioningly to bear its bitter disappointments, he or she must still wonder: Have I not confused a worldly-wise selfishness that can behave very respectably with true love that makes a human being really self-less and releases him or her to sink away into the incomprehensibility of God? Rightly understood, then, this *fraternitas*, this communion of brothers and sisters, is a very dangerous expression.

The Openness of Communion

A further consequence of a genuine communion of brothers and sisters—to be sure, along with a great many others just as important—is the transcendence of a sectarian mentality in our religious subjectivity. A Munich industrialist once announced that he was leaving the Church because the Bavarian bishops were seeking to add another holy day to the Church calendar, and he considered this to be economically unsound. His declaration demonstrated an utter failure to grasp what Christianity and Church are. Notoriously, they are only understood as a service to individual religious needs. Plainly, a communion, constitutive of Church, by which we come away from ourselves, take leave of ourselves, is not yet understood. For, once more, a communion of brothers and sisters will not after all be ultimately a matter of our own utility. It will lovingly affirm the other in himself or herself, above and beyond all personal utility, and thus mold oneness and, finally, Church, affirming this Church even (and precisely) where it is no longer of any personal advantage to do so.

Communion Within the Church

So we live in a world Church. And this Church is not simply tailored to our individual tastes. It does not suit the mentality of the neoindividualistic subjectivism of the twentieth century. Today there are people—Europeans in abundance, of course, but now Africans, Latin Americans, and others—whose mentality does not automatically fit in with our Western European neoindividualism, but who have the same right to a home in the one Church as we have. Whether we like it or not, their mentality works in the Church in such a way that we are affected by it ourselves. This may be uncomfortable for us, particularly when this foreign mentality unwittingly and naively presents itself as simply Catholic, quite as if it went without saying that it should be, when this is not the whole picture. A Polish Marian piety looks upon itself simply as part and parcel of the Catholic faith, hence as valid always and everywhere—and so it will seek to impose its validity throughout the whole Church, even though it may be in many respects foreign to our own sensibilities and arouse considerable resistance on our part.

Thus if we seek to live communion in the Church, this is something we shall have to deal with. After all, a communion of brothers and sisters requires precisely that we allow others the validity of their own mentality, even if that mentality is strange to us, and indeed even if it cannot, or should not, simply step forward in the name of the Catholic faith that obliges all. It is difficult to escape the impression that many of our young people today, while demanding radically more brotherly and sisterly communion in secular society, loudly protest what does not suit them in the Church, quite as if in matters ecclesial it were their perfect right to continue to practice a curiously old-fashioned individualism.

A thousand things in the Church do not suit us. This is perfectly plain. But why should they have to suit us? If the Church had to be just precisely the way we would like it, what would everyone else do? What would the Italians do—who, perhaps fortunately for them and for us, are less exact and mulish in juridical matters than we? What would the Latin Americans do, whose Marian piety is perhaps less observant of the theoretical limits of Christology than ours? Are we not, all unawares, objectively risking a shameless individualism and selfishness, with which we seek to live in the Church in such a way as baldly to arrange it to our own taste? When we feel, perhaps with some justification, that a bishop fails to "suit" us, do we still treat him as a brother, with whom we live in community for better or for worse?

Difficult as it may be for us, we live today in a concrete world Church, with its historical conditions and with the limitations and tentative character of the phase through which it happens to be going at the moment. Of course it has not yet reached a later, better phase. But it is in this Church that we must live. We must be prepared to abide an Italian curialism that for our brothers in Rome needs no explanation. And of course for our own part—for we, in turn, are their brothers and sisters—we too have the right to make our own desires, concerns, and troubles plainly known in this matter.

To speak frankly, quite a few German intellectuals in the Church find the Pope far too Polish today. But why should he not be a Pole? Why should he seek to perform the (ultimately impossible) trick of not letting his cultural origin show in his style of governing? There is simply no way for one's background not to have its concrete effects. On the other hand, to be sure, a view of things in the generosity of communion by no means obliges us to laud any and every administrative disposition a pope might make as if it were the ultimate stroke of wisdom, and the "pope fans" in the Church (may we be forgiven the expression) should not take it amiss if someone else in that Church, while unmistakably supporting the papacy itself, is less enthusiastic than they in these matters and honestly expresses some particular difference of opinion. This reciprocal tolerance, too, belongs to the intra-Church communion of brothers and sisters of which we have need today.

A Brotherly Digression

In this connection, we hope we may be forgiven if we inject a little something that perhaps does not pertain too strictly to our subject, but which we hope may make it easier for someone or other of our readers to come to an attitude of communion with regard to the pope and the papacy—which is not only a consequence of, but also a prerequisite for, a dogmatic conviction of the plenipotentiary prerogatives of that papacy.

It would not be difficult to imagine, in a genuine world Church today, within this global world history of ours that has become such a uniform, homogeneous history now, that the office of the papacy could assume an altogether novel and positive practical function, one which it has so far exercised in no concrete way, and which we perhaps instinctively seek today and fail to find elsewhere. Here will be something we can look to the papacy for, in hope and patience, as a concrete result and expression, here and today, of what we as Catholics believe about the papacy.

Specifically: Who today but the pope represents in a certain concrete, tangible, and audible manner the world conscience of a single humanity—a humanity today more than ever living in such a necessary unity? Here the question is not the theoretical limits within which we as Catholics may ascribe such a function to the papacy as a matter of principle. Here the question is rather to what extent such a function is, or can become, actually exercised by the papacy today.

Conversely, it is not as if a factual recognition of such a function were only possible on the part of those who subscribe to our dogmatic theology of the papacy. The function of such representation could be recognized as simply factual even by those who are not Catholics in the theological sense, just as, for example, a non-Christian may find the moral impact of the World Council of Churches meaningful for the non-Christian world.

We are not maintaining, with what we are proposing here, that popes today already adequately exercise this function of effectively representing a world conscience. But the papacy, more than any other authority in the world, does factually have this potential, and perhaps its actualization could be somewhat hurried along by our patience and prayer, as well as in other ways, so that gradually the pope, whoever he may be, may assume the function of representative of world conscience as never before, and be recognized in this function in many respects even by those who do not recognize the dogmatic function of the papacy. Something of the kind seems entirely within the realm of conception and desirability: the concrete concentration and tangibility of world conscience in this way, once recognized, would be most wholesome. It cannot be supplied by the United Nations. The concentration of interests and interest differences in UN world representation does not furnish such a conscience—it stands in need of one. Whether and how today's papacy could manage to assume such a function is another question. Certainly the papacy would need to present a clear image of itself not as the Patriarchate of the West, with its suffragan sees the world over, but unambiguously and right from the start as representing and supplying the principle of unity for the world Church as such.

As we have said it would be, this has been a digression on an opportunity for the papacy of tomorrow, and on a hope of ours for that papacy. It is only a little parenthesis, but it does have a bearing on our question of a communion of brothers and sisters—which Christians must have with the pope, too.

Christian Mission of Communion

A further consequence of today's new situation for Christian communion is the fact (and this may sound rather homely) that we Christians must all have something left over for the Church's world mission.

This world mission is a task to be performed in a different manner from the way it was carried out in the nineteenth century, when it exploited European expansion and colonialism for its own advantages (although it could scarcely have altogether avoided doing so). This goes without saying. Nevertheless, it is clear that today as well the world mission—evangelization everywhere—is and must be a task of the total Church in a world become one. And so our Christian communion of brothers and sisters does not stop with our next-door neighbor or the other side of the back fence. It must really be worldwide now, because the concrete situation of our communion today, whether we like it or not, has become a worldwide one.

It is equally self-evident that our Christian communion must not look only to the earthly well-being of our far-away neighbor—to right and justice in secular society—but also to the salvation of this neighbor in the proper sense, to his and her access to God's unconditional and infinite self-bestowal through the historical tangibility of Jesus Christ. Young Christians today seek a militant commitment to freedom and social justice all over the world, and it is well that they should. But they ought not to forget that this worldwide communion must surely not stop just where human beings' ultimate oneness begins—in God and his grace through Jesus Christ. It may well be that an explicit public commitment to freedom and justice throughout the world today is the first, absolutely necessary step for evangelization to take. It may be that this first step is only correctly taken when it is taken selflessly, without ulterior motives, as a simple deed of human communion among sisters and brothers. But none of this excludes the duty-in-communion of every Christian to undertake explicit responsibility for world mission and evangelization. Catholics should not be ashamed of this kind of interest in world mission, not even today. Their responsibility for the entire world must not end just where the execution of the ultimate mandate of their Church begins.

Social Dimension of Communion

A further consequence of a Christian communion of brothers and sisters as it must be implemented in today's situation consists in the insight that the very nature of this Christian communion necessarily generates a political responsibility, generates politics, and hence generates a political theology. Social, political responsibility, and our concrete perception of that responsibility—politics, then—scarcely need to be explained here. Nor need we enter into the dispute over what political theology is, whether it is necessary to have it, and how it is related to theology as a whole. Of course, when we actually come forward to take a stand for a particular political theology, or reject one, we have to say precisely what we mean by "political theology." Here, however, we may content ourselves with more simple considerations.

We have had till now a more or less static society, one which changed its actual structures very slowly, almost imperceptibly. Indeed one scarcely reflected upon the nature of this society, let alone its capacity for change or its actual changes. As a result, the tasks of Christian communion that were explicitly recognized as such were just as statically set, and hence restricted to a more or less private, or privatistic, relationship among individuals, and it was not difficult for them to remain that way. But now we live in a society that has made social and sociopolitical transformation the proper object of its very reflections and activity. We not only define our private existence in terms of a system of societal coordinates, we refuse to see that system of coordinates as fixed, and we change it. But thereby Christian love of neighbor and communion acquire a field of relevance they have never known: the field of the political, the field of responsibility for the social structures required for a life worth human living, a life that is "Christianly possible," in a society of maximal unification to this end. Today as never before, this responsibility can by no means continue to be borne by a few persons only. Today it makes its claim on everyone in a society. And the reason it weighs so heavily now, more than it did before, is that this responsibility must now be exercised in the context of a genuine choice among a multiplicity of simultaneous alternatives. It is no longer a matter of simple deductive intelligence. It is a matter of freedom, in itself and as such.

Thus politics today is no longer a matter only for "those in charge" as having an indisputable mandate from God. Today it is a matter of the responsibility of every Christian, albeit in a thousand different ways. Desirable as stability in sociopolitical structures may be, and with all due concern for the abiding validity of a basic legal structure, our new sociopolitical situation is ever one of becoming and change, and every Christian now has a political responsibility, even when the changes are occurring quietly and unobtrusively. We may therefore not allow ourselves to be deceived into thinking that the only valid Christian task is that of the defense of prevailing social structures and situations. It is perfectly possible, to be sure, for a Christian to be a conservative in some respect or other out of his or her inmost Christian convictions. He or she may be genuinely committed to the continuation of certain social realities from some basic theoretical insight, or indeed merely by virtue of a freely taken decision that is his or her own legitimate choice. In fact, a Christian may be very conservative and need not be ashamed of it. But we Christians may not act as if the dynamics of sociopolitical change were simply somebody else's business, and imagine that the defense of prevailing social structures, subject as they are (just as future structures will be) to sin, finitude, and human disappointment, is the only viable Christian task.

Presumably no one would actually espouse such a simple formula. But one easily has the impression that, subliminally, a broad undercurrent in the mentality of Christians simply assumes that we Christians are somehow automatically conservative. Has not all, or at any rate a great deal, of what has occurred since the Enlightenment first occurred in the face of bitter resistance on the part of Christians, the episcopate, or the pope? Is this simply to be explained as the fault of the novelty itself, in presenting itself tightly suited in the armor of expressions or ideologies that would inevitably and justifiably arouse Christian protest? Or does everything suddenly come clear when we consider, in Christian humility, that God's providence assigns us our special part in the cosmic concert, whose harmony is audible to God's ears alone, and that therefore we may not be allowed to protest the fact that, since the Enlightenment, the conservative counterpoint—which, after all, is also indispensable to the divine symphony of world history—has fallen to the lot of ecclesial Christianity?

Or would it not be best to leave aside all of these deep justifications of what was done sociopolitically by the Church and the majority of ecclesial Christians over the past two hundred years and tell ourselves, in a spirit of self-criticism, that the Church and practicing Christians in those times were not only laudably conservative, but often enough rigid and reactionary as well, and that a like mentality need not necessarily continue? If a (Blessed!) Vincent Pallotti said that Pius IX could see no further than his nose, and if we ourselves can have the impression that this pope was wiser in 1840 than in 1870 and ought not, after all, to have allowed himself to be led astray by the narrow-minded anticlericalism of the liberals of those days so that he abandoned his earlier attitude—then are we any less "good Catholics" if we seek to learn a lesson from experiences like these, and now try to choose more cautiously and broadmindedly among the various social alternatives available today in all areas of ecclesial and social life? Are we less good Catholics if we now permit ourselves a freedom of opinion, in a spirit of tolerance of sisters and brothers, in a better way than we did before?

This is the point at which the right to have a political theology arises. Political theology is not simply a social and economic doctrine in the old style, such as we used to have in the Church. Along with many another task it has taken upon itself to perform, political theology proceeds actually to interrogate theological teaching itself as to how spiritual-historical and sociopolitical systems and ideologies operate in the concrete, including this Christian social and economic doctrine itself as it has developed. This sort of questioning, bearing upon the totality of theology by way of a critique of ideology, is of itself something after the fashion of a political theology, and it legitimates it. For the rest, we need not concern ourselves with a more precise consideration of every essential aspect of the nature of this theology. We shall only say: It is yet another duty of a brotherly and sisterly tolerance to allow this theology to have its say. We may not reject it out of hand in a spirit of contentiousness that scents revolutionaries and modernists everywhere.

There are manifold instances in the nineteenth and twentieth centuries of the failure to criticize tacitly accepted social ideologies prevailing among Christians that had a disastrous effect on theology and ecclesiastical politics. Could a renunciation of the ecclesiastical state really only finally be managed under Pius XI?

Did the *Non Expedit* in Italy really have to be maintained all that length of time? Was Pius X's opposition to the trade unions in Germany really necessary? Did a theological integralism under Pius X have to entail such long-term and massive effects? Could a Teilhard de Chardin really not have been dealt with in a more brotherly fashion in Rome? These are the questions that arise, along with other, similar ones, in the background of the central question of the task and the legality of a political theology (little as we may restrict this theology to the area of the internal spiritual politics of the Church).

But the case may just as well be turned the other way about. Surely there are telling reasons for tolerance on the part of the representatives of a theology and a politics that deem themselves duty-bound to be on their guard against a theology and a politics in the Church that seem open to the indictment of ideology and reaction. These persons and politics, too, are under the obligation of a brotherly and sisterly tolerance vis-à-vis their adversaries. And this spirit of communion includes a calm, composed patience—an ability to wait, and to hope against hope.

Today's Christian has a political responsibility. It is an entirely new one. Surely there are offices and officeholders in today's society, as also in the Church, to whom everyone need not ascribe plenipotentiary sovereignty. But a communion of brothers and sisters today must be all the more strongly effective, precisely in view of the waning of an authoritarian mentality in the Church's concrete style of government. Respect for the Church's plenitude of authority rests on more comprehensive and more deeply rooted communion with one another than this in any case, for it is a communion through the same Lord, and one and the same grace.

Communion in the Parish or Local Community

The following consequences of our basic considerations bear mainly on the second aspect of today's situation: our new opportunities for intercommunication, our new routes of access to mutually shared subjective interiority.

We can have an altogether more intensive brotherly and sisterly communion today than we could in the past, through stronger bonds of intercommunication. Even in the area of the strictly religious, a brotherly and sisterly interiority have become not only possible, but a real need and obligation. Just consider how many people there are today who yearn for a "basic Christian community," or perhaps an "integrated Christian community." In these new kinds of quasi-parishes, one strives to build communities which go beyond the ones in which so many people have only their private religious needs fulfilled, through the ministrations of the Church in the Sunday liturgy, while persevering in their religious isolation from one another. In these new-style communities, people seek to bear life's burden together, in the company of one another, out of Christian motivation. Inspired by Christian ideals, people seek really to live together in brotherly and sisterly communion, to experience a oneness with one another, and actively to live out this oneness.

Of course, we must be on our guard against a certain sentimentality here—a longing for the simple life, and an inclination simply to copy the *comunidades de base* of Latin America. When illness strikes in the rain forests of Brazil, the only person who can help may be one's nearby brother or sister in Christ, because the physician or the hospital are too far away or too expensive. Here, then, of course, is a situation of brotherly and sisterly community, and truly "being neighbor" to one another as a duty of Christian motivation, that for us in our northern countries is not a practical affair, what with our doctor and our hospital right around the corner and a pocketful of medical insurance. In other words, in our countries there are clearly many services which elsewhere in the world may well be a matter for a basic Christian community, but which here are performed by secular society, and hence which scarcely come into question as something for basic Christian communities to do. But this does not mean that a lively Christian imagination cannot discover many a task of love, communion and self-fulfillment that a basic Christian community *can* perform among us. In an ever more anonymous and anonymously guided society like ours today, human beings are being forced to live in an ever more isolated fashion, in lonely helplessness and abandonment with respect to a good many of their needs and requirements, in which neither secular society nor today's average parish can come to their aid—needs and requirements in which neither money nor civil administration are of any avail, but only the heart of our brotherly or sisterly neighbor.

To what extent today's human beings will wish to go on living their modern individualism tomorrow, and to what extent they will voluntarily seek to be integrated into a basic community instead, is a question that has yet to be researched in these climes of ours. Presumably the problem will admit of a variety of solutions, just as in former times religious orders had very considerable differences among them, while they tend to be more uniform today. Even within a radically vital, genuine Christianity—and, to be sure, presupposing a radically vital and genuine secular society— many lifestyles are possible, especially in as much as the Christianization of human beings' respective situations will turn out differently in a context of a secular social differentiation of these human beings, and even Christian communion does not comport a priori demands for the egalitarian lifestyle of everyone in the parish or community. Presumably, then, the Church of the future will not be composed simply of integrated communities. But none of this alters the fact that today's situation makes greater communication possible and necessary in the religious area. We need basic communities too, and parishes must be transformed from units of authoritarian ecclesiastical territorial administration, and service stations catering to purely individualistic needs, into true communities, in which Christians live in a brotherly and sisterly fashion, united in the one Spirit who builds Church.

A Confessing Communion
The point we have just considered is surely a consequence and demand of communion that in turn implies another—a possibility we seldom see and take advantage of. We are referring to the duty of an uninhibited spirit of "joy of profession." Surely this is something that should be seen and exploited much more than it is now.

On the average, we are still religious individualists even today, and we have a very unbrotherly and unsisterly mentality. We have the idea that if there is any area of a person's life that ought to be locked up in the still, soft inwardness of the heart alone, it will be the religious area. Here, surely, we can have nothing to say to our sister and our brother. One can even gather the impression that such religious speechlessness is on the increase, even in religious orders. To be sure, there are examples of the contrary attitude, in the Church as in civil life. Extraecclesial religious movements and sects surely manifest a "joy of profession." Often they exhibit an uninhibitedness and brashness that may astonish and shock even those persons who do not seek to hide the light of their own Christianity under a bushel. But by and large, a strange religious muteness permeates our society, and it prevails especially where it is not upstaged by the arresting novelty of a rare or remarkable spirit of profession on the part of a few. How many parents are embarrassed to pray with their children! Where is there an uninhibited religious dialogue today, aside from the aggressive propaganda of the religious sects? Such religious dialogue is not "in" today. We are made uncomfortable by it. We find it out of place, and "indiscreet."

Such muteness, such inexpressiveness, is basically senseless. We must of course endeavor to speak of religious things in such a way that our discourse will have some measure of intention to be understood by and be relevant to our nonbelieving fellow human beings. This is difficult, and it is something that is not sufficiently striven for in the Church. The Church is too attached to traditional religious formulae, absolutely and exclusively, as if without them there would be danger of obscuring or losing the very substance of its faith and belief. Another thing we must avoid is the stentorian declamation of the inwardly embittered conservative reactionary, who risks using God to defend his or her bourgeois, middle-class status quo. But we can still foster a genuine uninhibitedness in our religious speech, a brotherly and sisterly openness and joy of profession, which would bear witness to, and seek to share with others, what after all is the inmost power and brilliance of our own life.

I recall something that once happened to me at the airport in New York. There in the swirl of humanity I found myself suddenly confronting a uniformed airport employee who approached me, knelt before me in the crowd, and said, "Bless me, Father!" Of course, we need not imitate this particular example of uninhibited piety, or ostentation if you will. But a spontaneous feeling of being permitted to share something of one's ultimate Christian motivation, something of one's fears and difficulties and blessings and happiness, with one's sisters and brothers, ought to belong to Christian communion even today, a communion both possible to us and enjoined upon us.

After all, in earlier times this kind of freedom of expression did prevail among Christians. It was not only in the confessional, or on the psychotherapist's couch, that one dared go outside oneself, dared to confide in someone else, dared to entrust oneself to another. Before his conversion, Ignatius Loyola was something of a wild soldier, with his amorous adventures and excesses of anger, rather a medieval type. It once happened that, having to take the field against the French, and having no chaplain available before the battle, he confessed his sins to one of his comrades in arms. We need not imitate him in this lay confession of his (even though at times such a confession might be just as spiritual and rich in blessings as sacramental confession, given the risk of the latter of degenerating into a legalistic formality). But this little example does show that Christians once enjoyed a spiritual intercommunication of brothers and sisters that was a good deal more open than it is today. It was simply accepted in those days—far more than it is today. Why need it be automatically suspect of indiscreet religious exhibitionism today?

If Christians have an inner piety, then they may of course be allowed to communicate it, to share it with one another, to whatever degree it may be meaningful to do so. There will surely still be different styles of such "confessing intercommunication" in the future. One person will be able to be more "joyful in profession" than another. But by and large such an uninhibited joy of profession in the Church today is something we hope will grow—among Christians, and on the part of Christians toward secular society.

There are still other, entirely different, neglected opportunities for brotherly and sisterly intercommunication, besides the ones on which we have been concentrating up to this point. If we still dare to ask someone to pray for us, for instance—are we still really serious about this habitual, traditional "request"? Do enlightened intellectuals, those still considering themselves Christians, really pray for their brothers and sisters? Or are our "assurances of prayers" for one another, and our requests for these prayers, no longer anything but fossil fragments from times gone by, things we keep handing on for custom's sake, but no longer seriously, from the bottom of our heart? Is a requiem mass for a departed friend or relative, if we examine it closely and honestly, more than a traditional ceremony of the sort that will continue to exist in a religious society even when the spirit and life are long since gone out of it? Tasks like these are but a few of the things that need to be done where spirituality and love of neighbor meet in the midst of daily living. There are sure to be many others. We have only to discover them.

Epilogue: The Mystery of Unselfish Communion

We have indicated a good many concrete opportunities for the practice of a Christian communion of brothers and sisters, or love of neighbor. And we have offered some wholesome advice for availing ourselves of these opportunities, banal and evident as our advice may often have seemed, and however much some of these things may already be enjoined upon us by sound human reason concerned with just getting on with the daily round. But before we conclude, let us weigh the mystery of this communion one more time. For that mystery is unfathomable. After all, even though it may be under only one of its aspects, it is actually identical with the totality of human existence.

Only in a communion of brothers and sisters is the human being genuinely encountered as a human being. A hostile encounter always deprives human beings of one another in an essential dimension, and makes them blind to this dimension. But the human being is ultimately a—no, *the* mystery. We are only ourselves when and where we trustingly and lovingly surrender, in freedom, in unbounded openness as the infinite question, to the incomprehensible mystery we call God. Thus the mystery of the human being is conditioned by and grounded in the mystery of God, but not ultimately via a thirst for a controlling knowledge and perception— rather only in the experience of the wonder of love.

One human being will be dealing with another in a love of neighbor. This love of neighbor will make the loving person over to the other, surrender him or her to the other, not simply in this or that surveillable and manipulable particularity (of utility, objective advantage, comfort in one's vital needs, esthetic infatuation, and so on), but as a whole—as "subject," as a person with an unsurveillable, limitless breadth of unbounded consciousness and concrete freedom, as a person who surrenders and loses himself or herself in abandonment to God. And vice versa: The beloved accepts the other in this love of neighbor, accepts the other as this incalculably mysterious subject. Love of neighbor is the compenetration of two such mysteries, in which Mystery *simpliciter*—God—is present and thereby ultimately renders all boundaries of these two subjects unrecognizable, inasmuch as at least what we Christians call grace makes God himself, as such, the inward determination of the finite subject, and thus God himself becomes an inward determination in both subjects' exchange through love of neighbor, or brotherly and sisterly communion.

Now, however, to these rather affective, mystical praises of the love of neighbor, we must at once add something basically and radically Christian—and something rather strange. There are other lofty anthropologies, or at any rate it is conceivable that such anthropologies could develop, in which the encounter of two such mysterious infinities in the infinite Mystery *simpliciter*—called God—could be conceived to transpire and be called love of neighbor. Thus such anthropologies would have the same sublime conception of the love of neighbor as in our own explanation. But such anthropologies, as ways of life, will always be in danger of understanding the actual occurrence of such all-embracing intercommunication between two infinite mysteries, this kiss of two eternities, as something that happens only rarely—something for which the normal life of everyday human beings can offer only feeble little practice sessions for the Lord of History, briefly undertaken by him only to be laid aside once more each time. An anthropology of this kind, undertaken on human beings' own initiative, will understandably dare to think of what it strives for and so energetically praises as something to be actualized in the lives of but a few saints, heroes, lofty sages, gurus, or mystics. Ordinary folk, the many, the all too many, will be hopelessly left behind. Such a sublime anthropology would seem to be inescapably condemned to elitism. It would seem that for the normal, ordinary human being, instead of this soaring brotherly and sisterly communion of infinite subjects, there remains only the eviscerated fraternization of a respectable common life, in which human beings communicate only in this or that particular conventionality and moderate gratification, not in their infinite subjectivity. This is understandable in the case of an *autonomous* anthropology of such sublime communion, for it can only reckon with the potentialities of the limited human being, and not with the power of God's grace and self-communication—which can actually make the infinite possibilities fulfilled realities.

The anthropology of a Christian communion of brothers and sisters knows differently. It has the unlikely courage to predicate the most improbable sublimity of the human being, and ascribe it to him or her as something possible, yet without becoming elitist. The Christian theology of a brotherly and sisterly communion is convinced that this communion of an infinite communication between two unbounded subjectivities, embraced and borne up by the absolute mystery of the infinite God, is possible for everyone who is human. Indeed it is convinced that it is not only possible for all, but that it is a sacred, inexorably enjoined duty—one for normal, average human beings as well, then, who ply their way through life, whose horizons seem dreadfully narrow, and who only appear to be driven somehow through the miserably narrow anxiety of their existence. No, a Christian anthropology does not fail to include even these. A Christian anthropology has the improbable optimism to assert that, even in these, the love a lofty anthropology praises, and can never leave out of account, can occur, must occur, and actually does occur.

When one considers the mass of human beings—how often they are frightfully primitive in human sensitivity, laboriously and heavily rolling through history like a great wave—one could easily be tempted to think, in skeptical resignation, that here if anywhere, in this mire of primitive instincts and selfishness, the miracle of this sublime love must occur but seldom indeed. But Christianity is convinced (and here we prescind from the question of infants dying before the age of reason, and other cases generically subsumable under this one, since, when all is said and done, we really know nothing about them, nor need we know anything about them for our purposes here) that, in each one of this anonymous crowd, to whom we ourselves of course belong, the unfathomable coming to pass of such love does take place, or else such a human being is lost entirely through his or her own fault.

This Christian optimism, adversary of all elitist insolence, has perhaps not sufficiently reflected upon how this wonder can occur in ordinary, average persons like ourselves. The matter of human beings' salvation has always been a legalistic one. Salvation and damnation are predicated on the fulfillment or nonfulfillment of a few individual commandments not actually having very much to do with the attainment of this supreme love of one another and of God. But this Christian optimism owes it to the faith-consciousness of Christianity to be anti-elitist, even if it does not know just how something it maintains as certain and unfailing can actually be conceived of as even possible.

But there are certain considerations which do indeed suggest, at least remotely, how such a miracle of tremendous love can take place in our seemingly so stale, miserable, bourgeois everyday lives. Such a miracle must be the deed of conscious freedom, of course. But it need not be reflexively explicit on the part of the individual, or accompanied by the deeply affective concepts which we have been unable to avoid using here—and which, for that matter, themselves fall short of the reality, which is always larger and deeper than can be expressed even in emphatic words like these.

Further: It is really quite comprehensible that, even in the life of the most ordinary person, moments should occur which offer space for such unreflexive, but real, love of infinity. Somewhere, even in the most normal course of a middle-class life (to which the whole of our cultural process belongs), there are moments in which that process calls a relative halt. It contains gaps and cracks —which look like empty fissures, but which, once we look hard, permit glimpses into the infinite. What seems to be the only reality then becomes just the starting point and framework for a gaze of awareness and freedom that loses itself in the infinite and no longer remains what one busies oneself with "soberly and realistically." More importantly: From time to time there seem to occur, in every human life no matter whose, moments in which the sober everyday love that can scarcely be distinguished from reasonable self-ishness suddenly finds itself confronted by the invitation to love without hope of requital, to trust without looking back, to dare to love where only a foolish adventure can reasonably be expected, one that "would never be worth it."

At such moments, human beings' freedom finds itself standing before the choice either of being cautiously cowardly—denying itself, and not daring to risk itself—or, in a foolhardy trustful-ness, seemingly absurd (and yet—wonder of wonders—there it is), of taking the risk, of risking our freedom and our free subject without looking back, of risking really loving in the proper sense of the word. There is no longer any ground to tap in advance to see if it is solid or not; then freedom dares more than is granted it by a calculating rationality, risks itself and its own subject, and plunges into the unfathomable, unbounded dwelling place of God, who can ultimately be experienced only in this bottomless, headlong plunge.

To be sure, this blind leap is ultimately occasioned, made possi-ble, and snatched up by what we call God's grace, which alone grants the freedom to take such an unconditional leap. But this in no way militates against the fact that a like miracle of infinite free-dom and love, and hence of a communion of brothers and sisters, can occur in the midst of the banality of everyday life. The launch-ing pad, if we may so call it, may be flimsy and narrow, and rise so scarcely above the flat plain of the everyday as to be hardly noticed at all. But these trivialities—the biblical glass of water to someone thirsty, a kind word at someone's sickbed, the refusal to take some small, mean advantage even of someone whose selfishness has in-furiated us, or a thousand other everyday trifles—can be the unas-suming accomplishment by which the actual attitude of unselfish brotherly and sisterly communion is consummated. And this com-munion is life's proper deed.

Christian faith is of the conviction that only love for God and hu-man beings, which is more than a commandment and obligatory exercise, brings human beings to salvation. It has the conviction that this love is the meaning of the whole of the Law and the Proph-ets, but that it can occur even in the humble, ordinary everyday—and that it is just there, in the everyday, unobtrusively, that the last renunciation and the last surrender to God can occur that admits us to a participation in the final deed of Jesus on the cross. A love of neighbor as one's brother and sister, a communion of brothers and sisters having a love for God both as its vehicle and as its consummation, is the highest thing of all. And this highest thing of all is a possibility, an opportunity, offered to every human being.